# RECOVERY OF MAN

# RECOVERY OF MAN

BY

## F. R. BARRY
BISHOP OF SOUTHWELL

CHARLES SCRIBNER'S SONS, NEW YORK

1949

# PREFACE

FOR several years I have wanted to attempt what is now attempted in this volume. Actually I did write a book with the same title in 1946 ; but on review it seemed so inadequate that sentence of death was tacitly passed upon it and I did not expect to find time to do it again. That, it appeared, was the end of that. Then came preparations for the Lambeth Conference and I was asked, amongst others, to put together some notes for the private use of the Bishops on the Christian Doctrine of Man. That meant gathering far more material than could be used for its immediate purpose, and that was worked up into the present book, which was written out very rapidly (as must, I fear, be obvious to the reader) in a few weeks before and after Easter. It is virtually a fresh composition and little of the first draft survives. Had I had the advantage, before writing, of listening to the discussions at Lambeth some of the views put forward might have been modified and others might be expressed rather differently. But the book was sent to the publisher in May and I next saw it in page-proof in August. For good or ill it remains as it was written.

The chapters that follow should not be regarded as attempting a full theological exposition but rather as indicating an approach. My aim is admittedly to defend a thesis—to stake out a claim for a humanist approach to the Christian interpretation of human nature. Too much contemporary theology and too much religious apologetic reveal an anti-humanist tendency which is, in my judgement, incompatible with the genius of Christianity. Any theology

v

at a time like this must be indeed a theology of crisis—and that note, I think, is not lacking in my treatment. But that is surely no reason for repudiating the great inheritance of Christian Humanism which has been the inspiration of Western Christendom. Because man's predicament is tragic, that is no reason for going back to barbarism. My desire was to make a humble contribution towards recalling Anglican theology to the characteristic Anglican tradition. Amid the insecurity of our time all the lines of opinion are hardening and " liberalism " is almost a term of abuse. We may recognise that some of the opinions held by pre-war liberal theologians were unsatisfactory or mistaken : but that need not be the same thing as formulating an " inhuman " and illiberal theology. I believe, for the reasons stated in the text, that Christianity is the real Humanism ; and because the Church is entrusted with the Gospel it is and must be the champion of man's cause. Christianity gives the real grounds for belief in man and hope for his recovery. For its centre is not in man, but in God.

What is now called the Western way of life has been essentially and profoundly Humanist. It derives in part from the Græco-Roman Humanism ; but this has been taken into and transformed by the distinctively Christian valuation of man as a child of God and heir of eternal life. From this flows that respect for human dignity and concern for the fundamental rights of man which the West is now summoned to defend against the assaults of barbaric ideologies. I am not so naïve as to think that " Western " and " Christian " are convertible terms. But there is such a thing as a Christian civilisation, in the sense of a culture which has been nurtured and guided by the Christian religion, of which these are the characteristic principles. That civilisation is now in mortal danger. It has drawn its power from Christian inspiration, and cannot revive or survive apart from it. The time has come when scientific Humanists and others who stop short of Christian theism, but care deeply for spiritual values and for the freedom and dignity of man, must ask themselves whether these can be maintained before the challenge of secularist materialism without the support of Christian faith and worship.

On the other hand, Christianity in the West has its roots in a cultural tradition which is now everywhere being undermined by economic and sociological pressures. If we want to see a revival of true religion—and there is no hope for the Western world without it—it may be that we must set about preparing the cultural soil in which it can take root. If there is to be a recovery of man there must be a re-birth of Christianity. If there is to be a re-birth of Christianity— which can come only by the gift of God—an antecedent condition on man's part may be a renaissance of Humanism, with its social and educational implications.

Some of the material now included in the sections which deal with education had been used already in addresses in College chapels in Oxford and London and in a University sermon at Cambridge. Dr. G. M. Young, who has recently published a valiant defence of the humanities, puts a similar point more picturesquely. " What the schools (he writes) have failed to teach is that a man has no more right to an opinion for which he cannot account than to a pint of beer for which he cannot pay " (To-day and Yesterday, p. 6).

After these chapters were in typescript there appeared the report of a weighty Commission presided over by the Dean of Winchester, on the Church's attitude to the Atom Bomb. Part of it covers some of the same ground and, oddly enough, in certain passages there is an almost verbal identity. That, however, is nothing but coincidence ; I had no contact with the Commission and had not seen its admirable report till this book was completed as it now stands.

It remains, lastly, to express my gratitude to two friends who helped me with advice and criticism, the Bishop of Bristol and Canon McLeod Campbell ; and to two never-failing secretaries, Miss Maud Joyner and Miss Pamela Jenkins, who have typed the difficult and scrawly manuscripts.

F. R. B.

MANESTY FARM,
BORROWDALE.
*August* 1948.

# CONTENTS

# RECOVERY OF MAN

## CHAPTER I

## THE CRISIS IN THE SOUL

"THE children are come to the birth," said an ancient king (Is. xxxvii. 3), "and there is not strength to bring forth." Is this to be the verdict on our time ? Whatever we may believe about the outcome of this ambiguous and daunting age, seldom, if ever before, can there have been so much idealism and goodwill thwarted by such frustration and moral impotence. Forces of life and forces of death are contending within Western society and within the soul of contemporary man. We do not yet know which of them will win, nor whether the revolutionary age is to end in the atrophy of the will to live and in mutual extermination. "Sometimes the period of change (said Whitehead) is an age of hope, sometimes it is an age of despair. When mankind has slipped its cables, sometimes it is bent on the discovery of a New World and sometimes it is haunted by the dim sound of the breakers dashing on the rocks ahead. The Fall of the Roman Empire occurred in a prolonged age of despair. Steam and Democracy belong to an age of hope." [1] To which does atomic energy belong ?

One of the salient facts of the present moment is the co-existence of hope with despair—but the former seems now to be waning rapidly. There are still no doubt millions who feed themselves on the revolutionary dream of better times and richer opportunity, even if in its crudest and most selfish form ; but considering people are more and more conscious of the sound of the breakers ; and it is ' dim ' no longer. Indeed a dreadful sense of foreboding seems to

[1] *Adventures of Ideas*, p. 7.

eclipse the light in our skies. Many believe that the night-mare is coming true and that civilisation is about to perish. If we all accept that belief, it will.

No civilisation is eternal. That theme runs all the way through the Bible from the legend of Babel down to the Apocalypse. There are only too many indications which may seem to point the contemporary warning, while the atom bomb is poised overhead. Apart from the economic anxieties and the darkening international situation, there are signs of profound spiritual malaise and deepening demoralisation. It begins to seem as though " Western man has exhausted the possibilities of the dream of mechanical power which has so long dominated his imagination," [1] and is now the victim of those external forces in which for too long he has put his sole trust. It is not merely that outward circumstances are increasingly difficult for us to master in a disorganised and stricken world. It is not merely that post-war fatigue seems to leave us unequal to the task. The Western achievement seems to have betrayed us. Some-thing has gone radically wrong at the heart of civilisation itself—some drying up of vital energy, some lack of incentive to recovery. Mr. Maurice Reckitt has lately drawn attention to " that great psychological failure of our culture, a failure so deep that its existence is still almost wholly concealed in the sub-consciousness of men—the absence of any hope of finding a normal satisfaction in the processes of their daily work. This takes the heart out of human activity." [2] Here we may be within sight of the real problem. Much more will have to be said about it later ; it is enough to suggest the possibility that our civilisation has now become exhausted.

No civilisation is eternal. But there is no inevitable decline and fall. We can at least spare ourselves the torture of a false biological analogy. A culture is a creation of spirit and does not merely pass through a life-cycle from birth to maturity and so to death. " Though all the other civilisa-

[1] Lewis Mumford : *City Development*, p. 132.
[2] *From Maurice to Temple*, ch. vii.

tions whose history is known to us may be dead or dying, a civilisation is not like an animal organism, condemned by an inexorable destiny to die after traversing a pre-determined life-curve." [1] The moral factor is the decisive factor. The formula of challenge-and-response which Professor Toynbee has made familiar is in true line with the teaching of the Bible, and is indeed in more modern dress the prophetic interpretation of history. It gives ground both for hope and fear. If it rules out historical determinism it also excludes any complacent optimism. It forbids us to think that we can muddle through or that Providence—as some of the prophets taught—will never allow Jerusalem to fall. It throws the whole weight of the decision on man's responsibility before God and on those moral and spiritual forces— the ' imponderables ' which realists ignore—by which alone history is redeemed. " The swift succession of catastrophic events on a steeply mounting gradient inevitably inspires a dark doubt about our future ; and this doubt threatens to undermine our faith and hope at a critical eleventh hour which calls for the utmost exercise of these saving spiritual faculties. Here is a challenge which we cannot evade, and our destiny depends on our response." [2] The question is whether there are still available recreative and renewing powers which can avert imminent disaster and give man promise of recovery. " When these things begin to come to pass then look up, lift up your heads, for your redemption draweth nigh." Can we in our day revive that expectation ? What has Christianity to say about it ?

Whatever it may or may not be, Christianity is the Gospel of the Resurrection. As such it is essentially faith in the victory of life over death, of goodness over evil and corruption. That is what it means to believe in the Living God. When the ancient civilisation fell, what the Church brought for its renewal was not a programme but a new attitude by which moral recovery was made possible—

---

[1] Toynbee : *A Study of History* (abridgement), p. 553.
[2] *Op. cit.*, p. 554.

essentially a ' conviction of new life.' That is the permanent and unchanging offer.

The primary mission of the Church at all times is to reveal the reality of the Living God and his purpose for the world of men, verified in those historical events on which the Christian religion is founded. Its message is proclaimed in indicatives—Here is the True Life, This God has done, God has spoken to us by his Son. Over all the world to-day there is famine—not of bread alone but of hearing the words of the Lord ; and the primary contribution of the Church to humanity in its terror and distress is to proclaim the word of God convincingly to our world of 1948. It will be inevitably a word of judgement ; for if God is ' faithful and true ' there is an eternal law of moral consequences—the ' wrath ' of God is one aspect of his righteousness. Once we forsake the first and great commandment there can be no stopping where we may want to stop ; and truth may be vindicated not least by the ruin that follows on its repudiation.

But it will be also a word of life and hope. No Christian can doubt that at the heart of history there are healing and redemptive forces able to turn failure to triumph. The day of the Lord may be darkness and not light ; but it is a day of the Lord nevertheless ; not a day of blind chance or of the devil. Not even in his most desperate sin or failure, not even at the crucifixion—there least of all—is man God-forsaken. History belongs to God, the Father of our Lord Jesus Christ. Christians, therefore, must not try to withdraw from it. We must not allow ourselves to be driven back into a kind of refugee-mentality. Our true place is rather ' on the frontier,' discerning and interpreting events in advance of their impact on society. It is for us to seek understanding of the forces now at work in the world, to make up our minds what in them is of God, which have and which have not seeds of life in them, which are the friends of man and which are his enemies. The answer will not be necessarily identical with that of conventional religious judgements.

The Church is not and never can be tied to any one

particular social system, and it may well be that this detachment is one of the lessons that has to be learnt afresh. Nevertheless the Church is in the world—not in the sacristy or in a vacuum—and it is in the world to redeem it. History is the element in which it lives. God's redemptive purpose through the Church can never be apprehended or obeyed in isolation from his ' strange work ' in those secular historical movements by which, at any given period, the Church's task and its mission are defined. It follows that at different points in history some particular elements in the Gospel, some aspects of Christian faith and doctrine, will be specially relevant to the world's need. It can hardly be doubted that at this moment the chief emphasis must be laid on that interpretation of the nature of man, which inheres in the Christian knowledge of God and the world-view which it implies. This is the crucial issue of our time. All other questions run back into this one.

This is indeed the core of the present crisis. We deceive ourselves if we think of it as merely a set-back or interruption from which we can soon emerge into ' normal times.' What we in this country had come to regard as normal— our material standards of life and our industrial primacy in the world—was in fact entirely abnormal, due to a combination of circumstances which are not in the least likely to recur. This is not a temporary crisis, nor is it primarily economic, though it has its stern and alarming consequences in the sphere of politics and economics. Fundamentally it is a crisis in the soul of contemporary man.

Politics at best can deal only with such relative and short-term remedies as public opinion is willing to accept, or conditions at any given time make practicable. The longterm problems lie far deeper down and few politicians in any party seem to have any real appreciation of them. They require far more radical diagnosis ; indeed the current political controversies only succeed in blinding us to the true issues. We do not do anything to save the ship by calling one another bad names—Tory, Fascist, Communist and so forth. These and other ideological symbols are but shadows, not substantial things. Nor, in fact, are these the real distinctions. The dividing line in the world to-day is not that between Left and Right, or between capitalism and socialism—these differences are superficial and may be said to be little more than verbal. It is between two ultimate philosophies, two interpretations of life, two answers to the question, " What is Man ? " All the other divisions run back into that one. Summarily, it is a choice between a theological or religious answer, with the God of the Bible at the centre of it, and a secular or Humanistic, with man, or chance, or nothing at all, at the centre of it. (A humanistic answer, as we shall see, always declines into an empty scepticism.) The conflict between two ways of life of which the war was one frightful episode, has now come to the critical decision. And it is the choice between life and death.

No external organisation can take the place of interior coherence, self-discipline and spiritual integrity. We are relying upon it far too much. If we try to lean upon it as a substitute for moral and intellectual re-direction we shall only accelerate the final breakdown.[1]

We talk big about a planned society, just at the time when we are most reluctant to ask, and least able to answer, the prior question, What is it to be planned *for* ? If we shirk that, our political directive can never be more than a shameless opportunism ; if we answer it wrong, we are planning for disaster. But this is the question—What is man and what is the end and purpose of society ? What does human life really *mean* ? Behind that, is the theological question ; and most of the urgent questions of the hour are

---

[1] " A failure to respond to a challenge successfully is the essence of the catastrophe of social breakdown, which cuts short a process of growth and gives rise, in its place, to a process of disintegration. A disintegrating society is failing *ex hypothesi* to respond to a challenge that is presented to it ; and so long as the challenge remains unanswered it will continue to hold the field."—Toynbee : *op. cit.* (original form), vi., 280.

unanswerable apart from theology. A theological answer to the question means setting it in the framework and context of a God-centred world-view, such as has in the past been the constant background of the European and Christian culture. On a secular or merely empirical basis there is no possible answer to the question other than the limits of power to enforce the desires of one group on another. For there is no ultimate court of appeal ; no absolute truth and no moral law.

Here we find what in the following pages we shall encounter several times again—that the whole idea of law, and therefore of freedom, is significant and practically effective only through a religious understanding of the world and human life within it. The ' assertion of the validity of law ' and ' the uncompromising tradition of the moralisation of power ' have been constant and characteristic elements in the legacy of Western Christendom.[1]

The West is now making the experiment, perhaps the first in recorded history, of trying to build a stable society without any acknowledged world-view ; no society can survive on those terms. The contemporary ' substitute religions,' false and destructive though they may be and are, bear witness at least to that necessity ; and one of the discoveries of our time is that ' dogmas ' passionately believed are what liberate energy, whether for good or ill. " Whatever the nature of these beliefs they appear to perform an essentially social function without which no society can long survive. In degenerate forms they may poison a whole culture ; in a healthy form, compatible with contemporary knowledge, they will inspire its greatest achievements. . . . The attempts of eighteenth- and nineteenth-century rationalism to do without such motives and create a society of calculating, rational individuals was doomed to failure." [2]

However little ' Christian ' it may have been in conduct or in personal discipleship, there has been a distinctive type of

[1] J. Bowle : *Western Political Thought*, p. 147, 194 and passim.
[2] J. Bowle : *op. cit.*, p. 19.

Christian culture which has been bound up with the Christian world-view. The Gospel has not been its only source. The cultural inheritance of the West was not exclusively Christian in origin. It incorporated vital elements preserved from the legacies of Greece and Rome, and Christianity has not the slightest interest in wanting to minimise these contributions. The Christian ethic is not ' purely ' Christian. It rested upon insights gained already by the classical moralists and philosophers as well, of course, as the Jewish law and prophets. Cicero's ethical treatise *de officiis* was one of the textbooks in the Christian schools, and St. Ambrose adapted much of it for his own use. The passages in the New Testament Epistles which expound the principles of Christian conduct include a good deal of ' common form ' material taken over from pre-Christian sources—a fact which has only recently come to light through the researches of biblical scholarship. So, again, the concept of *lex naturae*, so normative in the Christian social ethic, was originally propounded by Stoicism and worked out in the Roman law of equity. There can be no need here to dwell on the dominating influence of Aristotle in the formulation of scholastic orthodoxy.

Many other traditional elements were taken over and worked into a coherent whole, held together, sustained and unified within the totality of the Christian world-view and beneath the over-arching Christian theology. In the process they were, to a large extent, transvalued and baptized into the service of the Gospel. The basic assumptions of this Christian culture were trust in the rationality of the universe, the supremacy of the moral law and the essential dignity of men as the inheritors of an eternal destiny. Thus, under whatever political regime, there was inherent in it throughout, the sense that government is a moral trust to be exercised on behalf of the governed, and always, therefore, at least the germ of freedom. (The latter was also in part the contribution brought into the ancient provinces of the Empire by the social and political institutions of the northern barbarian invaders.) This culture, established in the West, which is now no longer a geographical term, has been the parent of all the highest achievements of civilisation up to the present time. For the West it is what ' civilisation ' means ; and with all its failures and blemishes it has, under God, been a very noble thing.

The unanswered question is whether it can survive. Is Christian civilisation to continue with liberty and compassion in its veins ? Or is this in truth the post-Christian age ? There is still far more of the Christian tradition, alike in thought and in practice, among our own people than in any other of the Western countries. Yet here, as elsewhere, we are now in real danger of breeding a new type of human being—not Western Christian man as history knows him, but ' hollow men ' with no inner life, wholly concerned with external and material things, while the empty citadel of their souls is hag-ridden with fear, frustration, resentment— and cruelty.

Christian civilisation has rested on that valuation and understanding of the nature and destiny of man which belongs to the Christian world-view as a whole. Various elements of it still survive, torn out of their theological context. All preserve some fragmentary truth, but in isolation are dangerously misleading. The breakdown of the medieval synthesis left a highly intricate work of architecture—which we have since elaborately enlarged—with an immense variety of detail but with no controlling principle of unity. When the theological centring was removed there was nothing left to hold it together save what has been called the ' desperate expedient ' of the modern nationalist state. Life has become in the literal sense distracted—pulled at once in many different directions. Alike in society and in individuals it is fragmentary and disintegrated. The soul of man is divided against itself, and that inner discord is reflected in the disorganisation of society. We are constantly trying to plaster up the cracks but the building is radically fissured. Our deepest need is spiritual wholeness, and the key to any social restoration is to rebuild the inner soul of man. Yet man apart from society is nothing. We can only be whole men in a whole society. And the achievement of a whole society requires a ' whole ' philosophy of life. That is precisely what we no longer have.

It has been destroyed from within. One of the most unexpected developments in a civilisation which claims to be ' scientific ' has been a headlong, Gadarene ' flight from reason.' This has made way for a corroding scepticism which is threatening the whole Christian legacy. Mr. Lewis Mumford remarks very quietly, and as it were in a meditative parenthesis, that " it was not in the bloody operations of the Guillotine in 1793 that the forces of revolution and disintegration showed themselves most clearly. . . . No, it is in the apparently innocent lucubrations of David Hume that the real Reign of Terror began ; the beginning of nihilism which has reached its full development only in our own times. In his *Enquiry* the assault on historic filiations and human reason reached a pitch of cool destructiveness. Hume used the technical processes of Reason to sap its very foundations." [1]

What has come to be called the age of reason was, in fact, the age of its renunciation, for rationalism warns off the field whatever is not immediately intelligible. Thus it can never understand history, and has only the most jejune appreciation of those mystical, undefined intimations by which both men and their societies live. Leftist thought about social problems still tends to be rationalist and atomistic. It thinks society can be manufactured instead of taking a long time to grow. And therefore it tends, unwittingly it may be and unaware, to be anti-libertarian. (It is not for nothing that the Great Leviathan was begotten out of seventeenth-century physics.) Revolutionary thought despises history. Progress tends to be thought of in terms not of getting nearer to a goal but simply of getting further from a starting point —from all the accumulation of experience and all that society has been becoming. All the revolutionary movements in

---

[1] *The Condition of Man*, p. 269.

Europe since 1789 have consistently followed the same pattern.[1] However intense and bitter their fanaticism yet always, by an ironic paradox, there is cold scepticism in their vitals. This scepticism is the root of tyranny and of the demoralisation of our times.

If men once abandon trust in Reason and in the objectivity of Truth, they are playing straight into the hands of tyrants, whether Fuhrers or impersonal collectives. Free government then becomes impossible ; for if there be no absolute truth there can be no objective standard by which the acts of the State can be criticised, and indeed no common language in which the community purpose can be expressed. Rational thinking and objective criticism are drowned in a flow of irrational propaganda ; and Truth degenerates into ' political truth '—i.e. the party-line of the dominant group. This is the pragmatism of dictatorship : *Hoc volo, sic jubeo ; sit pro ratione voluntas.*

Moreover, the abandonment of absolutes swamps ethical standards in relativity. There is then no ultimate court of moral appeal to which the earthly state must be subject. The new-model post-Renaissance state claims to be the source of its own law and its own moral justification,[2] and this is the lie in the soul of the modern West. Moreover, each national or party group now claims to be absolute in its own right, claims in fact to be a ' mortal god '—merciless, all-demanding and capricious. There can be neither justice nor freedom without the recognition of a moral law which all acknowledge and by which all are judged.

Thus intellectual and moral relativism—now generally described as ' nihilism '—is the food on which the tyrant state grows. It has been found, and will more and more be found, that it is when faith in God and in man's eternal

---

[1] " An imposing alliance between three different forces came into being through the events of the French Revolution, and has never been broken up since : the alliance between irreligion, Utopian hope and compulsion. The outcome of this combined secularist venture has been so far not an earthly paradise, but something very different—the modern State."—Meissner : *Confusion of Faces,* p. 63.     [2] Cf. Bowle : *op. cit.,* p. 194.

destiny grows weak, that the absolutist state waxes strong till it usurps the sovereignty of God.

This nihilism grows like a cancer till it sets up mental and moral paralysis—that inability to believe in anything and that abdication of responsibility expressed in the phrase " I couldn't care less " which is the fundamental and final atheism. This is the gravest danger which threatens us, and, unless it can be overcome, must lead to total breakdown and anarchy.

Thus the heart of the crisis is religious. The rather glib superficial Leftism which controls the popular mind at present, with no thought-out philosophy behind it and no recognition of that unseen background from which true social health derives, will never be able to stand up success-fully to the impact of its fanatical competitors. It is vain to suppose that the characteristic values of Christian civilisa-tion can survive on the basis of any secularised world-view, or on that basis resist the challenge of Marxism by which all non-Christian thought and secularist experiments in ' Democracy ' will, in all probability, be devoured.[1]

Indeed we cannot insist too emphatically on the intimate and necessary connection between political and social move-ments and theology or world-view—or the absence of it. It is not now possible for Christian thinkers to study or to expound Christian doctrine without sociological implications. There is only one radical and consistent social doctrine in the world to-day outside Christianity, and that is Communism. All that is happening lays it upon the Church to think out afresh its own specific doctrine concerning man and the ends of society which has always been inherent in its theology. It is not least because it has neglected this that the world is now haunted and bedevilled by the rivalry of ideologies, each of which claims to be absolute and exclusive.

---

[1] " The central problem of twentieth-century Europe is to decide whether the moral and political ideas, resting on the conception of liberty and law as complementary to each other, which are now held in common by Christians and Humanists, can be rationally sustained on other than Christian grounds."— *Times Lit. Supp.*, January 31, 1948.

The Gospel is not about man's ideals, still less about his failures and betrayals—as some of its heralds now seem to think—but about the victory of the Living God. As such it is the answer to our predicament. It comes " to satisfy the empty soul and to fill the hungry soul with goodness." The demoralisation of the West is due in part to physical conditions, on which there is no need to enlarge here; and Christianity does not underrate them or the extent to which their improvement—e.g. by the export of coal to Europe— would contribute to the recovery of morale. But its funda- mental cause is not material: it is due to spiritual mal- nutrition. Men know of nothing real in the Universe—no ' bread of reality ' (St. John vi.) to feed their souls; and ' starving men will eat anything, even poison.'

Because they are starved they are losing heart and hope. Trying to create a new social order out of their own desires and ambitions, men are crushed with the feeling of helpless- ness and suspect all principles as wishful thinking. To believe in God means, at the very least, that there is a Truth to be known and a Goodness to be reverenced and served, that Justice and Love belong to the nature of things and are neither ' relative ' nor illusory. Christian faith means that the living Goodness, the reality of a spiritual universe, draws near to man in self-disclosure, to lift him out of his loneliness and frustration, to strengthen his weakness and redeem his failure, and admit him to share in the creative purpose. Therefore it is good news for man and hope—a ' living hope ' in a despairing world—and the one guarantee for the survival of human values in a society drifting fast towards disintegration. Our society perishes for lack of it.

" Without hope and without God in the world "—the phrase describes the contemporary sickness. The disintegra- tion of Western civilisation is exhibited most clearly and most terribly in the dissolution of Hitler's Germany, and it is one of the ironies of history that Germany in defeat is far more dangerous than ever it was in the days of its armed might. The whole West is handcuffed to that corpse; the sepsis has entered the blood-stream of Europe and none can be immune from that contagion. But what happened there was the fatal end of a sickness long endemic in civilisation, gradually mounting to its climax.

Christians take a graver and more tragic view of it than the purveyors of ideological nostrums. They offer no magic panaceas. It is not too hard to cure some of the symptoms ; it is not too hard, rather it is too easy, to create in the masses of the people a delusory sense of material health and well-being. The disease remains and cannot be ' healed lightly.' We may be sure that healing and recovery from this morbid state will take a long time—*and we do not know whether time will be allowed us*. If (as Christians should be) we are realistic, that spectral doubt haunts all our calculations. But we do know that whatever short-term remedies (in all of which we are eager to co-operate) may help to stop the spread of the disease or alleviate the painful consequences, the only true and lasting cure is spiritual, and that new life can be imparted to us only by the word of the Living God. Recovery for man means recovery of his divine birthright and inheritance.

Human values are everywhere threatened. The course of the world seems to be pitted against them. The spirit of man to-day is in prison, and we do not know how to break a way out. We are fighting bitterly on unreal battlefields, blinded by ideological obsessions. It is like that last battle in the West where

> Friend and foe were shadows in the mist
> And friend slew friend not knowing whom he slew.

But the real fight is not against flesh and blood, it is against principalities and powers and the world rulers of this darkness. And did they but know it, all men everywhere are together on the same side in that battle. If there is to be an uprising of man and a reassertion of the human against the sterile tyranny of process, the servitude of sub-human valuations and the dark dominion of evil, that can only be by man's rediscovery of his true nature and status in the scheme of things. That can come from the knowledge of God alone. For there is no guarantee and no security of man's status and dignity as man, apart from his relationship to God and the gracious activity of God towards him, which is the perennial message of the Gospel. All other attempts to give his life significance, to interpret to man the enigma of his experience and invest his little day with eternal meaning, lead but to contradiction and despair.

That is happening now. It has happened already before. It was into a psychological situation strangely and frighteningly like our own that the Christian religion first came. The Hellenistic age might be described, like ours, as an age of Humanism *manqué*. The proclamation of the gospel of God in the ancient world had as its result the re-affirmation and re-vindication of the status and dignity of man. The New Testament is the charter of man's dignity. For lack of a valid philosophy to justify it or a credible religion to sanction it, the Hellenistic culture was beginning to turn back on its heritage of Humanism and losing confidence in its own assumptions. The spirit of man was breaking under the strain of trying to uphold human values without belief in a God to guarantee them. The statuesque, classical tradition of *humanitas* was proving itself inadequate to carry the burden of its own ideal. So that world was growing demoralised, falling into despair and superstition, abandoning its trust in rationality, becoming incapable of creative effort. What Christianity brought was not a programme of political or social reformation, but faith in life itself, in God and man ; and that made a new spiritual climate in which creative solutions become possible.

The Gospel rehabilitated man. It set his life in the grand dimensions—the length and breadth and height and depth—of God's purpose for him in Christ Jesus. It lifted man to a dignity and status immensely and unimaginably higher than Sophocles or even Plato dreamed of, as the child of God and the heir of life eternal. It ennobled the ' weak and despised things of the earth ' with a heavenly calling and a divine destiny. When man was dwarfed and human life was cheap, the gospel reaffirmed the Psalmist's claim that man was ' crowned with glory and honour ' and invested him with a royal majesty. Christianity told men and women what they are—" heirs of God and joint-heirs with Christ " (Rom. viii. 17). Against all that impugned its rightful title, all that cast doubt on its intrinsic worth, all that cheapened, corrupted or abused it, the Church stood forth as the champion of humanity. It declared that men were ' ends in themselves,' not means to, nor instruments of, anything. And all this rested finally on the Gospel, on that re-valuation of human life which was implicit in the Christian faith in what God has done for man in Christ. Man is incommensurably precious because God loves him and Jesus died for him and the Spirit can, in the full sense, ' make a man of him.'

It was this re-affirmation of man's dignity which redeemed the outcasts and reclaimed for their divine destiny and birthright the victims of cruelty and exploitation, and eventually set free the slave. It was this which, amid the anarchy of the dark ages, when the classical civilisation had gone down, was able to vindicate human values against ruthless and destructive barbarism and to keep alight the lamps of spirit in the night of brutish ignorance and savagery. Here is the core of Christian civilisation and the permanent guarantee of Humanism. It is guarded by Christian faith in God and a God-centred philosophy of life—i.e. by a religious interpretation of the nature and destiny of man. Still to-day it is the Christian Church which is (and will more and more be found to be) the one effective bulwark of the human cause in a world in which it is in mortal danger.

## CHAPTER II

## PREFACE TO HUMANISM

IN the war of spiritual liberation, to rescue man from his degrading servitude to those dehumanising forces which threaten to deprive him of his birthright and defile everything that ennobles manhood, what allies have we to count upon ? Who are the friends of man and who are his enemies ? In the ever-narrowing strip of no-man's-land between the high religions and secularism, are the light and scattered patrols of Humanism, attempting gallantly to defend man's cause, yet without supplies or reinforcements and under no organised command. Unless they are re-formed and embodied within the Christian lines they will melt away and be rapidly overwhelmed by the enemy.

For it is on the Christian side that they belong. It might seem to betray a strange lack of insight when Christian apologists denounce Humanism, even in its all-too-human forms, as an enemy to be attacked. It is a weak ally to be succoured. It is, as might be said, like Vichy France, temporarily weakened and wavering, yet essentially the friend of the liberators. Much of our current apologetic literature is, in my judgement, ' getting it all wrong.' This chapter, though it may seem to some readers to lean over too far in the other direction, is written as an attempt to correct the balance. It is not merely an academic point. If the Church is to rally the forces of goodwill, if it is to baptize into the faith of Christ whatever may be still vital and creative in the flux of the world situation and build from its elements in dissolution a new form of Christian civilisation, then it must at least know where to look for them. It must not—

to change the metaphor abruptly—try to disfranchise its
fellow-travellers or liquidate them as counter-revolutionaries.

The Gospel and Humanism [1] belong together. The
creation of a humanist culture is indeed the genius of
Christianity. In all places since the first beginning, the Gospel
has verified its power to liberate and enrich the life of men
and invest it with ' more than its original dignity.' It is
not traditional Christianity but emancipated ' modern
thought,' which takes a low view of human nature. The
quarrel of Christianity with Humanism (in its usual contemporary meaning) is not that its claims for the spirit of
man are too high, but that they are not high enough, because
it leaves out the reality of God and the gift of eternal life
by which man's value and status are *conferred* upon
him.

But that is no trivial omission! It involves radical and
far-reaching differences, not alone in the respective attitudes
of Christians and Humanists towards religion, but also in
their ethical valuations. It would be quite misleading to
suggest that the moral principles of Humanism are identical
with those of Christianity, lacking only theological sanctions
or the reinforcements of religious practice. Just because
they are *not* theological, just because they *are* ' humanistic,'
the moral values and judgements of Humanists are bound to
differ widely from those of Christians—as they often do at
quite unexpected points. Christian spokesmen are frequently
accused of having ' betrayed ' supposedly Christian principles
if they do not endorse the arguments of pacifists, or sentimental theories of punishment, or if they take a stern and
exacting view about the obligations of marriage—a view
which is said to be ' unkind ' and ' un-Christian.' But the
fact is that because Christianity values life by the measure of
eternity, and interprets the nature and destiny of man in

---

[1] In the sense of ' devotion to human interests ' (O.E.D.). The idea is
well expressed in the title of Sir E. Barker's charming book, *Traditions of
Civility*, published after this chapter was in type.

terms of its relationship to God, Christian ethics are not just ' humanitarian.'

What is to-day commonly known as Humanism [1] is in effect an attempted half-way house between the Christian world-view and secularism. It has manifold varieties of expression, impossible to catalogue here in detail, and different intensities of religious overtone. It ranges from the exquisite refinement of Gilbert Murray or H. A. L. Fisher through the positivism of H. G. Wells (who was perhaps in his popular appeal, the most influential writer of his time) to the anti-God propaganda of the Rationalists—as they so paradoxically call themselves. It is not necessarily irreligious. It frequently uses Christian phraseology. It often speaks of ' spiritual values ' and reveres Beauty, Truth and Goodness. It acknowledges a high sense of moral and social obligation, the claim of non-material satisfactions, and of devotion to the common good—mainly in the form of ' duty to posterity.' It often evinces a religious temper and in such representatives as Julian Huxley it professes to be itself a religion, but expressly a ' religion without God.'

It is the ' religion of all sensible men '—so tolerant, so non-mysterious, so ' free from the trammels of sectarian dogmas,' that liberal, cultured minds can give allegiance to it without compromising their independence. It is indeed a ' liberal ' *tour-de-force*—a Christian temper without Christianity, a defence of man's spiritual inheritance without belief in a spiritual ground for it. (A Marxian might plausibly describe it as a kind of religious epi-phenomenon of those pre-1914 conditions which underlay political Liberalism). What it is, in fact, is a kind of Christian heresy. As Christian eschatology was taken over and turned into secular Utopianism without God or the hope of life eternal, so Humanism has tried to make its own the moral and cultural values of Christendom while abandoning their basis in theology.

[1] In the sense of " any system of thought or action which is concerned with merely human interests as distinguished from divine " (O.E.D.).

Here, perhaps, we may find the common denominator.
All forms of contemporary Humanism take for granted an
immanentist philosophy.    They are anthropocentric not *MAN - CENTERED*
theocentric, so that there is a contradiction at the heart of *GOD-CENTERED*
them which brings them all in the end to bankruptcy.
Humanism in all its many varieties is avowedly ' humanistic,'
man-centred.   Art, ethics, religion, are regarded, not as
response to a God ' outside ' ourselves, but as creations of
man's moral consciousness, innate spirituality and ' idealism.'
Mingling with popular evolutionism and the Victorian belief
in progress, engendered by the industrial revolution, this
has gradually taken shape in the current secular world-
view—the belief that by more science, more technology,
better education and social conditions, men will ' move
upwards, working out the brute ' and establish a man-made
' paradise on earth.'   This is the ' religion of the modern
man.'

It may be both arrogant and superficial, and the facts of
contemporary experience are a damning commentary enough.
But the right Christian reaction cannot be a negative, anti-
humanist polemic.   That is to point the road back to the
jungle and repudiate the whole Christian legacy as well as
all the harvest of civilisation.

Christianity was not born in a vacuum.   In its nature it is
historically conditioned.   On the stream of its historical
development the Church has brought into the Western legacy
a rich inheritance of pre-Christian culture.   Christianity has
taken over all that was best in the insights and creations of
' classical ' art, literature and philosophy and baptized them
into its own life.   (Whether Greek metaphysics are, in fact,
compatible with the ' personalist ' form of Christian theism is
a question which we shall meet in a later chapter.)   It
incorporated them into its ' body.'   Whatever may be the
case in the mission fields, where the Church must now, for
the first time, incarnate itself in non-European culture-
patterns,[1] so far, at any rate, as concerns the West, there

---

[1] Stephen Neill : *Christ, His Church and His World*, ch. v.

can be no going back on them. All these gifts of Graeco-Roman Humanism now belong to the *philosophia perennis*, and are permanent elements in Christian culture. The tragedy was that the Reformation, particularly in its Lutheran form, in the attempt to recapture the ' pure ' Gospel, uncontaminated and undefiled by ' catholic ' and non-scriptural accretions, repudiated this grand inheritance. Thereby, however unknowingly and unwillingly, it began to destroy Christian civilisation.

Thus increasingly since the Renaissance these elements in Christian Humanism have become <u>divorced from their theological context</u> and asserted a claim to validity in their own right. With the new knowledge and the new discoveries and the ever-developing technical inventions, <u>man has seemed to himself no longer dependent on a God who transcends him and his world</u>, and has <u>claimed for himself the last word in the universe.</u> Man (as has been said) ' makes himself,' and the God-hypothesis is no longer necessary. This is the assumption of all modern Humanism, and to the mind of a Christian it is blasphemy.

*[margin note: Assumption of Modern Humanism]*

But we must not for that reason turn our backs on all this great cultural tradition, or reject our heritage in Western Christendom. Whether in its ancient or in its modern expressions Humanism enshrines precious values which no religious temper can underrate. The insights of Plato, Sophocles and Virgil are real insights and we must not disown them. The achievements of the spirit of man in the arts and sciences are real achievements. There has been, and is, genuine moral progress—despite of all that now shouts denial. <u>If man is made in the image of God, the Creator, then the human spirit is creative and expresses its nature in creating.</u> <u>Christianity accepts all this because it sees in the victories of man the self-revelation of God to man and in him.</u> Within the framework of the Christian world-view and a God-centred interpretation of the nature and destiny of man the positive valuations of Humanism receive validity and authentication. Torn away from a

theistic world-view they prove in the end to be self-contra-
dictory. For then there is no ground for absolute values, no
guarantee for the status of spirit. All becomes relative and
in the long run meaningless.

The trouble about a man-centred creed is that it cannot
long remain man-centred. Only too quickly it will fall
victim to the consequences of its own negations. Inevitably
it degenerates into naturalism and falls down into scepticism
and despair. Classical Humanism found that out, too late
to arrest its own decline and fall, and the same thing is
happening to its modern version. For the humanistic substitute for Theism has cut away just those presuppositions
which it had unconsciously taken for granted. If man really
is the ' crown of things ' Humanism itself becomes untenable.
For it is not permanently possible to retain belief in spiritual
values apart from belief in transcendent Spirit as their
ground and their guarantee. There can be no mental or
spiritual quality in the constitution of the universe unless
there is Mind or Spirit at the centre of it. This is what
Humanism has denied, it is the inherent self-contradiction
in the axioms of non-theistic Humanism. Unless we believe
in something higher than man, Humanism cannot be defended
and man drops to a sub-human status.

For there are in the humanist world-view no reliable
defences of spirit. We have only to mention four names—
Darwin, Freud, Einstein and Marx—to remind ourselves of
what in fact has happened. Submerged in the processes
of nature, alone in a vast and terrifying universe, conditioned
by social and economic pressures, man can no longer assert
his claim to lordship. The next stage could never be far
away. Anti-Humanist forces get control and the human
cause is brought into mortal danger. Hermann Rauschning
indeed has declared roundly that " men are only humane
when they do not make themselves and their aims the
centre of their system, but subordinate it (sic) to that which is
higher than man. Humanism is thus a first step towards
de-humanisation because it makes man his own judge and

himself the end and aim of life, recognising no judgement of a transcendental authority." [1]

A further paradox, always implicit in the humanist position, has now declared itself.  If there is indeed nothing higher than man, then he is alone in the universe, the sole champion of the human cause, with no higher source of confidence and renewal.  Some fine minds have been able to find here an ennobling sense of call to a high vocation and a dedication to responsibility.  " We are alone, we must not betray the trust."  But what can we do when we know that we have failed it, and what can repair the damage of our failure ?  That is the question that haunts the post-war world, and a purely immanental philosophy of nature and history can give no answer.

It is, moreover, only the elect few who have been able to see things in this light.  For most, the very claim for man's uniqueness has had the paradoxical effect of diminishing and dwarfing the human stature.  For this lonely eminence is frightening.  The popularisation of the sciences revealed a universe vast and ever vaster, ever more machine-like and impersonal, which seemed the very negation of spirit and utterly unconcerned with the human experiment.  Against the dark backward and abysm of astronomical time and stellar space it was more and more difficult to maintain that man really mattered in the universe.  Man now seemed dwarfed into insignificance and acquired the status of a ' displaced person ' in what all the time is his Father's house.  Men are losing confidence in themselves and find a queer masochistic pleasure in the veneration of the ' little man ' as the totem-symbol of their unimportance.  Yet this, we are told, is a time for greatness !

Thus man becomes dwarfed in status and significance, a part of nature and unimportant at that.  Human pretensions come to seem ridiculous and we have a literature of dis-illusionment.  On the top of all this the lives of men and women have been blasted and shattered during these last

[1] *The Beast from the Abyss*, p. 7.

ten years by the manifestation of naked evil, apparently
using good as its tool, and against it they feel impotent and
powerless.  Hence the appalling sense of futility, the mood
of cynicism and despair, which is rotting the vitals of the
civilised world.  Man is shown up and the human cause is
lost.  This, after all, is the ' fate of *homo sapiens*.'  The
experiment seems tp be ending in a debacle.  Utopia proves
to be more like Hiroshima.  Men are losing confidence in
humanity and are left with nothing else to believe in.

This is the so-called Bankruptcy of Humanism, and
Christian spokesmen are perhaps too ready to claim this as
proving their own case, or as the defeat of an ambitious
rival.  If Humanism is indeed bankrupt, then it is a disaster
for the Church no less than for the survival of civilisation.
When men lose faith in their humanity—which is a real
danger to-day—civilisation is under sentence of death ; it
will be destroyed by ' internal barbarism.'  If civilisation
reverts to the jungle (as it easily might) where will the
Church be ?  The contemporary breakdown of Humanism is
indeed nothing for Christians to gloat about ; Humanism is
our friend, not our enemy ;  and when all human values are
threatened Christians and Humanists need one another.
The great task of the Church in this savage era is the
rehabilitation of Humanism.

The whole Bible stands for ' human values ' against all
that debases and corrupts them.  In the grand vision of
Daniel (ch. vii), for example, the barbaric, ' imperialistic '
powers are symbolised in animal and sub-human forms—the
lion, the bear, the leopard and the ' great beast.'  Upon them
the judgement of history is passed ;  ' their dominion is taken
away.'  The living God gives sentence against them.  The
Kingdom is given to the people of God and to ' one like unto
a son of man.'  The advancing purpose of God in history is
thus identified with a human figure ; and in fact the Hebrews
were ' out of the jungle ' a long time earlier than the Hellenic
peoples.  The significance of the book of Daniel—the first
attempted philosophy of history written in terms of the

biblical world-view—for Christianity cannot be overestimated. When Jesus was born to be the Christ—the centre of history— its faith was vindicated. The God-man is the saviour of Humanism and the man-God will always be its destroyer, as has been seen again and again in history from Old Testament times to the present hour. (The ' mortal god ' is Leviathan the great beast.) If the Church is to play its true part in the redemption of this post-war world and not be overwhelmed beneath its ruins, it must be as the champion of man and the protagonist of Christian Humanism.

Conversely there are certain pre-conditions of any genuine Christian revival, so far at any rate as concerns the West. The drift away from religious conviction is due not less to sociological pressures than to moral failure or intellectual scepticism. It is possible for men to be so ' conditioned ' by their environment and its suggestions as to become just non-religious and apparently incapable of religion. There can be a kind of spiritual soil erosion, so that Christianity cannot take root and grow ; or the thorns may spring up and choke it. Something like this seems to be the case now. If we look for a rebirth of religion, we may first have to set about preparing the cultural matrix to receive it. The redemption of civilisation by religion and the pre-training for a Christian world-view in the great masses of our population by a revival of humanist culture, may indeed be regarded as two moments of a single interlocked enterprise which is the task of this generation. All men of goodwill must work together to revive the inherited values of civilisation which are, as Christians believe, God-given to man.

The Church is now faced with a situation for which it is not directly responsible, but within which it is desperately hard for the values of civilisation to survive or for the Christian religion to expand. Both what is called the climate of opinion and the social and economic trends of industrial civilisation are inimical to the higher activities of spirit. The fact is perhaps less glaringly apparent in this country at present than elsewhere, but even here the rot has already gone deep. A secularised material civilisation of uniform type, both outwardly and inwardly, is fast sweeping over the whole world. Everywhere it has the same 'gadgets,' the same clothes and radio and films and the same external apparatus ; everywhere the same mental outlook and the same interior emptiness of soul. Wherever it goes it takes with it sterility of spirit and seemingly also of population ; it cheapens and depersonalises men and defiles the image of God in them. Christian civilisation can survive only if it can 'fight back' effectively against this latest barbarian invasion.

The Church must be at the heart of the Resistance ; and the victory can only be achieved by a penetration in depth, as well as by that numerical extension, which is now described by the 'blessed word' Evangelism. A country with a number of Christians in it is not the same thing as a Christian country. But it is unrealistic to imagine that the Church alone can throw back the tide. It must work not only by its own methods and in its own distinctively religious field. It must also win the trust and collaboration of all men and women of goodwill who are ready to go with it any part of the way, and work with them through 'secular' agencies, whether governmental or broadly cultural, for the restoration of our threatened values.

No 'appreciation' of the whole campaign could possibly be written by any one man. There would seem, however, to be two points in a single interrelated enterprise with which the Church must be specially concerned and to which it can bring a peculiar contribution. These are, the rebuilding of community and, in the widest sense of it, Education. In real life they are interdependent, and there must be a certain artificiality in attempting even to think about them separately.

(1) There is clearly a causal connection (though it may be a two-way causality) between the drift away from religion and that disintegration of community which has followed upon the industrial revolution. The drift away from religious

conviction is indeed only one among many consequences of a
collective drift away from reality.  The great majority of our
population do not merely take their opinions and their scale
of values at second-hand, they are themselves living at
second-hand.  The vast urbanised agglomerations into which
men and women are now herded, in an ever-more gregarious
individualism, reduce them simply to units or points in an
immense involuntary system in which individuals no longer
matter and personal qualities are at a discount.  This
' megalopolitan culture,' as Lewis Mumford calls it, becomes
a colossal and intricate mechanism for turning out substitutes
for direct experience.  The astonishment of evacuee children
at discovering that milk comes from cows, not out of tins
from the chain-store grocer-shop, is indeed a typical illustration of the falsification of life in Megalopolis.  Everything
that men feed upon is ' processed '—not only their food, but
their daily work, their art, their thinking and their recreations.
" The mischief is not due solely to the physical ills produced
by a wasteful and over-complicated urban routine ; it is
due to a growing concern for the inessential, the trivial, the
glamorously empty, which Paul of Tarsus found, in a similar
period of decay, among the Corinthians and Athenians.
This wholesale perversion of values is fatal to life."  Therefore
the name of the city is Nekropolis.[1]

This mass-produced contemporary life is the fertile breeding ground of irrationality.  There is no significant pattern
of experience in these depersonalised human aggregates and
but small scope for purposive activity.  There is little indeed
to suggest that life ' makes sense ' or to strengthen the
feeling of need that it should.  The sense of neighbourhood
has been swallowed up and people no longer ' belong ' where
they live.  It is not uncommon on the big ' estates ' (or for
that matter in blocks of luxury flats) to find that people
cannot tell you the name of the next-door family or the
adjoining street.  There seems to be no organic social
relationship ; the crowded life flows on around but nobody

[1] Mumford : *The Plan of London* in *City Development*, pp. 174, 172.

seems to have any real share in it.  All the decisions seem to be made by ' them ' ;  men and women do things and suffer things independently of their own volition.

Such conditions breed, almost inevitably, an irrational and fatalistic attitude.  To-day it is only a very small minority who are capable of consciously thought-out reasoning.  Advertising rests on the assumption that ' anything goes ' if you say it often enough. .People are at once sceptical and credulous, and are only too easily exploited by mass-suggestion and high-power propaganda, whether by politicians or pill-vendors or anti-God orators in the Park.  This appalling danger to ' Democracy ' is also the gravest impediment to religion.  For the enemy of religious conviction is not thought-out and reasoned agnosticism but the passive credulity of the vacant mind.  Here is indeed the seed-bed of nihilism ;  irrational superstition grows apace in it.  The cult of Astrology seems to be spreading rapidly.  People, apparently otherwise intelligent, carry about mascots and talismans.  A further symptom, socially more disastrous, is the raging fever for gambling, more and more shamelessly commercialised, which is playing such havoc with national character.  This appears to be one of the constant symptoms of the disintegration of the social structure, and the parallels from Rome and Byzantium are so haunting as to make us shiver.  This is part of the established ritual surrounding the worship of the goddess Luck.  And it is one of the clearest indications that men have no longer a foothold in a common life which offers them any framework of coherence or any suggestion that life has a purpose.  Minds that have been conditioned by this atmosphere cannot even begin to ask the questions to which religion offers to give an answer.  This mental barrier to communication is the fundamental problem of ' evangelism ' ;  and religion alone cannot hope to penetrate it.

On the other hand, this gregarious loneliness produces deep psychological injury and is probably one of the un-acknowledged causes of what men mean when they talk about frustration. It easily tends to the mood of the *enragé* and inspires revolutions of destruction. Recent events have shown very forcibly that beneath this atomistic mass-society there is an intense craving for community, which modern man must and will secure, if not in a true form then in a false. It is a humbling thought that Christianity has allowed Communism to ' get away ' with the word—which is primarily a Christian word—and with its own horrible version of the thing. It thrives most vigorously in a social vacuum. Christianity cannot resist it alone ; we must build around it centres of resistance, economic, cultural and social as well as spiritual and religious. The Church's most effective contribution, both for its own cause and for the cause of freedom, is to perfect its own local embodiments of creative personal *Koinonia* in the parishes and congregations. Any parish anywhere in Christendom that is building up a significant community of worship and life is performing a vital service both to civilisation and to the Christian mission. Hence the immense importance of the country parish (see below p. 45). And short of that, on the pre-Christian level, anything that is done by any agency, religious or secular, which helps people to feel that they have roots in a common life and belong to a society which needs them, is beginning to stem the tide of demoralisation.[1]

(2) Turning now to the field of Education, we may first recall the elementary fact that we cannot be educated in a vacuum. Many philosophical reformers have drawn up ideal schemes for education, planned to turn out ideal citizens as architects of an ideal society ; but they have been intolerably abstract and have stood in no organic relation to the social or cultural background and environment of those whom they were planning to educate. The trouble is, there is never a clean slate. Education at any given time inevitably, and within limits rightly, reflects the aims and the ruling values

[1] See the Church Assembly Report, *Towards a Common Life* (1948). With the bibliography.

and indeed the 'whole climate of opinion' of the social
order within which it functions.  It is and should be its
deliberate aim as a civic and communal activity to hand
on the social tradition from one generation to the next.
And it cannot transmit what it does not possess.  Thus
for any educational reform the problem and the key to it
(if there is one) is with adults rather than with the children.
To follow this up now would take us too far.  I am only
concerned here with the obvious point that the social
field and the educational field have no defined frontier
between them.    The tendencies which we have been
examining in the disintegration of community have their
effects in the educational system ; while there are in
the educational system tendencies which accelerate the
breakdown of community and generate a 'climate of
opinion' which is antipathetic to a religious world-
view.

But it would be merely defeatist to conclude that because
there is this 'vicious circle' there is therefore nothing that
can be done about it.  For all this is only another way of
saying that you cannot chop life up into bits and pieces.
And after all we have got to start somewhere.  If we want
to stop the oncoming hosts of barbarism, then we must try
to organise defences whenever there is a foot of ground to
stand on.  Education is in the front-line defences ; and it is
a terrain which the Church knows intimately.  The Church
cleared this field and has tilled it for the better part of a
thousand years longer than any other agent now at work
there.  But if we would save Christian civilisation, we must
realise that here, too, as elsewhere, Christians cannot do this
job alone.  In the contemporary situation much of what needs
doing must be done by political or official action, and therefore
by political or official methods which are and must, in the
nature of things, be sub-Christian.  So if we want Christian
education it is not only the 'religious' values in education
that have to be defended, but the fundamental educational
values.  We must be concerned not only for religion but

for education itself.[1] There are certain defects in it which must be remedied, and trends in it which must be reversed if it is to become an effective instrument for the rehabilitation of Humanism. And unless they are, Christian education will become increasingly impracticable ; it will be choked by the atmospheric pressure.

Before we can hope for a human recovery, to say nothing of a revival of Christianity, we urgently need a return to trust in Reason. The modern West claims to be ' scientific,' but it is in fact rotted with superstition. " There are many people (says Professor Ritchie) who think that because science can do astonishing things it can do anything and everything, and that science is the whole of civilisation. A civilisation wholly scientific would be a contradiction in terms, because science is necessarily a part of something else, not the whole of anything." [2] But a part of what ? At the least of faith in Reason, based upon the two-fold conviction that the Universe is in its nature rational and that the human mind is a valid instrument. If that is not so, there can be no science. If we cannot or do not trust reason, we cannot think about anything at all, and any statement that anyone cares to make is as true and therefore as false as any other. In practice, of course, every form of scepticism makes an exception in its own favour. There is no truth to be known —except this. All rational judgements are determined by sub-conscious processes—except Freud's. Philosophy is no more than a by-product of economic conditions—except Marxism. This in itself shows that if we start by questioning the validity of Reason, we can make no statement at all beyond the assertion—This is how I feel ; and even that cannot be claimed as ' true.' Yet this is precisely what we have been doing, till an age dominated by the science which is one of the greatest achievements of Reason has been

[1] I fully agree, of course, that in the long run, no Christian can accept that distinction ; from our point of view, education which is not religious is just not education ; but this form of words may be admitted here for there seems to be no other way of saying it.

[2] *Civilisation, Science and Religion* (Penguin), p. 9.

characterised in its latest phases by a growing tendency to irrationality.

It has shown very little understanding of the forces at work in our time and of its real needs that too much religious apologetic has evinced an anti-scientific bias. If either religion or science are to survive what we really need is a great deal more, not less, of the true scientific spirit.[1] It is only by this that people can be protected from irrational and dangerous mass-suggestion, which can overwhelm scientific objectivity together with social order and freedom ; this alone, in the religious sphere, can liberate their minds from the tyranny of unquestioned and unexamined slogans— ' Religion has now been disproved,' and so on. Moreover, we need a rebirth of rationality for the restoration of our moral standards. For there is a two-way interaction between Reason and the Moral Law. Belief in an objective moral standard, on the one hand, is bound up with trust in Reason ; while, on the other, science is bound up with the recognition of reverence for Truth as an absolute moral obligation. In the Western social tradition the two lines converge in Jurisprudence. Under totalitarian regimes Justice and Science alike are corrupted and made ' procuresses to the lords of hell.'

But there is also another side to all this. It was said by one of the ablest of our bishops—Dr. Herbert Williams, formerly of Carlisle—in a speech in York Convocation, that ' before there can be a revival of religion, there will have to be a revival of great poetry.' Anyone who understands what he means by that will understand the point I am trying to make now. It is, no doubt, a convertible proposition ; for we cannot have great poetry or great art without a deep background of religion. All great art hitherto has been religious ; in the sense at least that it could take for granted a fundamental religious tradition in the community out of which it grew. Coterie-art, engaged in a private game in which the public are not invited to join, is art divorced from

---

[1] Cf. J. E. Jessop : *Evangelism and Education*, pp. 19–20.

a religious setting. We have gone so far to-day in disintegration, in the isolation of ' religion ' from aesthetic and intellectual experience, that it hardly occurs to contemporary artists
that the Christian tradition of faith and worship has anything
significant to say to them. Poetry needs a revival of religion
as much as religion needs a revival of poetry.

We may remind ourselves here that the Church, as the
trustee of Christian civilisation, has a cultural mission to
discharge, in addition to, yet indeed as part of, its own
pastoral and prophetic ministry. Alike on cultural and on
religious grounds it must have a constant, eager ' concern '
for art and literature and creative craftsmanship. If
Christians are to be in the world like salt which preserves
civilisation from going bad, this surely applies to aesthetic
and intellectual no less than to moral and religious values.
If we want to stand out against triviality and to raise the
standards of appreciation there must be a new, vital interpretation of beauty and dignity in Christian worship—neither
of these means elaboration—bearing fruit in graciousness of
living. One can hardly think of anything more unpopular
that any ecclesiastic could say—but it is possible to go too
far in the ' democratisation ' of the Church. Perhaps indeed
we have gone too far already. Not everything traditional
is ' reactionary ' ; not everything dignified is anti-social ;
nor is everything ' democratic,' Christian. We can only
create a people's Christian culture through an aristocracy
of a new kind, which has nothing to do with ' privilege ' or
income. That is what the Church should be creating, what
indeed the Church itself ought to be.

But what, precisely, did Dr. Williams mean ? Perhaps
we can explain that from another source. Baron Van Hügel
used to advise his penitents and others who sought his
spiritual guidance, to read, not the literature of piety, but
a stiff course of history and classics—Homer and Virgil,
Plato and Thucydides. He was never tired of insisting that
the soul needs to be purified and strengthened by the cul-
tivation of mental interests which are not in themselves

technically 'religious.' He would say, I think, that the study of classical literature, permeated with the quality of *Humanitas*, was a true preparation for the Gospel. People who have never taken time, or have never been trained, to reflect on the splendour and tragedy of man or the mystery of human life and death, have never seriously asked the great questions to which Christianity offers them the answer. It is ' hardly ' that such minds can enter the kingdom of God. People who wish to predispose their minds towards understanding a religious world-view may well be advised to initiate themselves by pondering over the Shakesperian tragedies, which could have grown only out of Christian soil.

Thus part of the resistance to neo-barbarism will be the restoration of ' the humanities ' to their rightful place at the centre of education. We need to recover what C. S. Lewis has called ' the immediately sub-Christian perceptions and virtues, the rich Virgilian or Platonic penumbra of the Faith.' [1] If so, we must resolutely set our faces against the fatal contemporary dualism between ' liberal ' and ' vocational ' education. This country needs more and more technicians ; but it will be disastrous if men and women are trained in engineering and applied sciences, but with no humanist educational background and no understanding of the records of man's intellectual and moral experience as they are enshrined in the humane studies. There are far too many B.Sc.s about who are semi-illiterate and half-educated. Pre-occupation with the merely technical produces a kind of gadget-mentality, with no concern for the ' causes of things,' no capacity for sustained thinking, no appreciation of spiritual values. This is de-humanising in its tendency and is bound to be anti-religious in result.

The Convocation of London University has put on record its profound misgivings about the growing tendency to ' divorce between humanistic and scientific studies.' [2] All Educationalists indeed must share it. But this cannot be

---

[1] Preface to *How Heathen is Britain ?* p. 13.
Cf. correspondence in *The Times*, August–September, 1946.

rectified by a Royal Commission, such as London University has proposed. It is not a problem that can be solved on any purely administrative level. It is bound up with our whole understanding of the nature and aims of education. And the fact is that during the last century education even here in England, to say nothing of other Western countries, has been in danger of losing its bearings and becoming uncertain of its own objective. Secondary and higher education have been falling into bits and pieces, labouring under an ever vaster weight of specialised knowledge, unrelated to any centre of unity or aim ; and that inculcates a philosophy of life which has no centre of meaning or significance. The question, What is a University for ? will receive no confident or convincing answer ; for a total philosophy of education presupposes a total philosophy of life, and that is what we conspicuously lack. The time has come when it must be recognised that we cannot teach politics or art or history or science or literature or anything else, if we leave theology out of the reckoning. Theology is, and must be again admitted to be, the synthesis of education.

It has been said that " the attitude of the Churches to the founding of the modern Universities in England . . . was one of the most disastrous failures of Christian responsibility in our history." [1] The statement is capable of a wider reference. If the Church had claimed for God's service the new learning of the sixteenth century, if it had sought to baptize into Christ the new biology of the nineteenth century, or the new physics of the twentieth, how much alienation and estrangement from the Christian faith should we have been spared to-day ! What ruin and tragedy might have been avoided ! Both the Church and the universities are paying dear for that fatal blindness. It will need great insight and humility on both sides to overtake the consequences. We must have collaboration on a new basis to rescue man from his spiritual bankruptcy.

We can, I think, no longer afford the luxury of what has

[1] Daniel Jenkins : *The Gift of Ministry*, p. 125.

come to be called ' useless knowledge ' *simply as an instru-ment of mental training*, regarding the construction of a world-view or a standard of ethical valuation as a purely personal and private matter.  That was a prevailing academic attitude at the time when the late Professor Collingwood (who was as it happens, an exact contemporary of mine at Oxford) was an undergraduate.  His own comment on it is worth quoting —" The inference which any pupil could draw for himself was that for guidance in the problems of life, since one must not seek it from thinkers or from thinking, from ideals or from principles, one must look to people who were not thinkers (but fools), to processes that were not thinking (but passion), to aims that were not ideals (but caprices), and to rules that were not principles (but rules of expediency). If the realists had wanted to train up a generation of English-men and Englishwomen expressly as the potential dupes of every adventurer in morals or politics, commerce or religion, who should appeal to their emotions and promise them private gains which he neither could procure nor even meant to procure them, no better way of doing it could have been discovered.  The result of all this might have been even worse than it has been." [1]

It has been assumed that in order to be ' liberal ' Educa-tion had to preserve a strict detachment from the positive dogmas of religion and remain neutral about the ultimate questions.  Therefore Theology had to be excluded from any official place in the course of studies.  You could ask all questions in heaven and earth except the question What does life mean ?  You could prove the falsity of all religions—that was a mark of freedom from prejudice ;  but to suggest that Christian experience could merit serious consideration was the mark of an illiberal sectarianism.  That prejudice took a hundred years to die, and its ghost is not yet com-pletely laid.  However liberal in its intention, that policy, as we can now see, has been obscurantist in result.  It has in fact imposed another dogma on the mind of two genera-

[1] *Autobiography* (Penguin), p. 37.

tions—an outlook on the world and on human life to which, for all academic or practical purposes, the reality of God is quite irrelevant. And it becomes increasingly apparent how that mental vacuum will be filled.

Christians have now thankfully to recognise that official academic policy is breaking away from these old fears and prejudices. Many of our civic universities have now established Departments of Theology ; University College at Nottingham is the latest to take this enlightened step. The provision for instruction in Christian knowledge written into the Education Act as the basis of the national system, goes further than anywhere else in the modern world. But a further step remains to be taken and it is exceedingly dangerous and delicate. It is not enough to recognise Theology as one subject of study among others, whether in a school or a college. Theology to be worthy of the name must become the co-ordinating focus of its intellectual wholeness and integrity. If that wholeness is not found in a total world-view, then obviously it cannot be found anywhere. The delicacy of the problem, however, concerns the question of academic freedom. Truth is one, and all truth is of God. If the Christian religion is true, then there can be no kind of knowledge which is not related to the knowledge of the true light that lighteth every man. Moreover, intellectual integrity and impartial scientific objectivity depend, in the long run, on the acceptance of high ethical and religious standards. " Low general moral standards of any kind might destroy the scientific tradition. Respect for truth and respect for persons as part of the general social tradition are needed for science to survive. Historically these come to us through the Christian tradition." [1]

All this and more may be rightly insisted upon. Yet it would be disastrous and fatal both for Christianity and for Education if there were even a hint of interference with the rightful autonomy of the other disciplines, any attempt to pre-judge their findings or to work towards an edifying con-

[1] Ritchie : *op. cit.*, p. 170.

clusion.  There must be what Maritain would call Pluralism
within the whole of the Christian world-view.  But to find out
exactly what this implies and just how it works out in
practice is one of the biggest educational problems for the
restoration of a Christian culture.  It proved to be too much
for the Middle Ages.  We need imperatively to find the
answer.  We have yet to find out more exactly what is the
vocation of a Christian student or teacher of economics or
biology, or any other ' non-religious ' subject ; and what
under contemporary conditions is meant by a ' Christian '
school or university.  Obviously it must mean something
more than one which happens to have Christians in it or even
one of which all the members are Christians.[1]  To this there
is no slick and facile answer, but it is hardly possible to
exaggerate how much depends on finding the right answer.
It can be found only by experiment.  The long-term and over-
riding need is the re-education of Western man into a theological world-view, a God-centred philosophy of life, which
claims all knowledge and every human interest for the service
of the true and Living God.

Christians and Humanists need one another.  Christianity
alone can safeguard Humanism against degeneration into
secularism in which ' human values ' are destroyed.  " Time
may well show, if it has not already shown, that Christianity
alone can preserve and guarantee the true status of man." [2]

[1] On this, see Nash, *The University and the Modern World*, and Brunner,
*Revelation and Reason*, ch. xxiv. and xxv.
[2] E. G. Selwyn : *I Peter*, p. 77.

## CHAPTER III

## GOD AND MAN

WESTERN civilisation as we know it has been built on certain valuations of human life and beliefs about society which, although (as we have seen already) they derive in part from the Graeco-Roman legacy, are ultimately Biblical and Christian. This whole tradition is now in mortal danger. It is one of the tragic ironies of history that the defeat of the Hitlerian challenge to it has left it so dangerously weakened, so perilously exposed to a new menace, both from within and from without, that its very survival is an open question. This is at last becoming clearly recognised. Thinking people have become aware that the Western ' way of life ' can survive only at the price of eternal vigilance and a steadfast will to defend it. This carries with it strategic implications which they are reluctantly ready to accept, no less than resolute and decisive action in the political and economic field. What is not yet adequately realised is that no external defence can save it if the inner spiritual citadel is left ungarrisoned or has been betrayed.[1]

Neither for Christian thought nor in history has the *status quo ante* any survival-value. The inheritance of the West can survive only by a re-birth and revival of those distinctive spiritual values, those interpretations of man's task and destiny, which it owes to the faith of Christianity.

---

[1] " The active barbarians in our society were aided by the passive bar-barians who had lost their hold on the central human values, and saw no reason to risk pain or death on behalf of human ideals—for ideals had become empty words "—Mumford : *The Condition of Man,* p. 368.

There is no other source from which they can be renewed. It is easy to talk big about defending them, but more important to know what they are.

For as to that, we are muddled and confused—too ready on the one hand to identify the prevalent social aims with ' Christian ethics,' too prone, on the other, from the Christian side, to withhold any religious recognition from what is best in contemporary thought, on the ground that it has not been baptized. ' He that is not against us is on our part '— Christian and Humanist or (as the *New Statesman* likes to call it) ' civilised ' thinking can travel some way on the road together. But whereas, if the Christian partner is not there Humanism is left down and out, Christianity can go on alone. It has its own insights to guide it and its own resources to uphold it. What they are, and what illumination they can bring to some contemporary problems I shall attempt to consider in this chapter.

The Christian understanding of man is through and through theological and religious. This of course does not mean that it is ' dogmatic,' in the sense of being entirely *a priori* and impervious to new factual evidence. But what it does mean is that it is God-centred. Accordingly, though it must welcome and accept the proved findings of investigation, whether by the physical or the social sciences, into the natural history of man and the evolution of his culture, its total interpretation of the facts will always be distinctive for this reason. It approaches them all from a different standpoint and within a God-centred frame of reference.

The Christian doctrine of man derives from and depends throughout on the Christian doctrine of God. What man is, whether simply as *homo sapiens* or as inheritor of eternal life, he is by the ordinance and gift of God. All science, however impartial and objective, starts out from an act of faith of some kind ; it must at least know what it is looking for, on what principles it is collecting evidence, before the facts can mean anything at all. If we start by believing, as

Christians, that ' what it is to be man ' essentially is to be a creature made in the image of God, it follows that the account which will be given of his biological origin and behaviour will not indeed tamper with the facts in order to point an edifying moral, but it will be different from the account given by anyone who assumes that man is simply and solely a biological species. From this standpoint one could almost justify speaking about a ' Christian Biology '—it is not what Samuel Wilberforce would have meant by it. (This is no merely academic point. It is of great practical importance for the presentation of the Christian ethic. For example, instruction on sex enlightenment setting out the so-called facts of life from a purely biological point of view may be positively misleading from a Christian one.)

The foundation of all Christian thought about the world and man's place within it is the sovereignty of the Living God as Creator and ruler of the Universe. It is this which distinguishes between the Biblical and Christian interpretation of the world and any kind of immanentist world-view, whether that of popular evolutionism or of philosophical idealism. God transcends nature and history ; all that is is dependent upon him and exists to serve his sovereign will. This is the central conviction of the Bible and the presupposition of the Christian world-view, and is taken for granted in our Lord's teaching. The unique contribution of the Prophets was to recognise that the sovereign will is Righteousness ; so that the physical structure of the Universe is essentially related to its moral order. Both are expressions of the Being of God. The God who is known as sovereign in conscience is the God who ' made Orion and the Pleiades '—maker of all things visible and invisible. The whole created order is a unity— this is the first axiom of the sciences—and the ground of the coherence is moral. Such is the setting and context of man's life. " Man in the Christian as in the scientific view, is part of nature, having his own place in the one great scheme which is the plan and purpose of the Creator." [1] The Bible

---

[1] Temple : *The Church Looks Forward*, p. 79.

records the developing apprehension of the character and content of that purpose through the self-communication of the Living God to the minds and consciences of men, mediated through the history of the Hebrews as interpreted by the insights of the prophets, verified and fulfilled in the coming of Jesus Christ and in the faith and experience of the Church. If the Christian religion is true, it is not merely the truth about religion, it is the truth about life itself—about God and Man and the nature of the Universe, and the goal of human institutions.

It may fairly be said that the Christian doctrine concerning the nature and destiny of man is implicit in the words of the Creation myth : God created man in his own image (Gen. i. 37). Whatever may or may not be true about man, nobody claims that he is self-originated. He depends on something else—but on what ? Right back here, at this crucial road-junction, the various creeds and philosophies diverge. The Bible ascribes the ground of man's existence to the volition of the Living God, the Lord both of nature and of history : ' it is he that made us and not we ourselves.' As created, man is part of ' the creation,' in the sense of the evolutionary process—the birth of the stars, the emergence of ' life ' and the ' entropy ' which will end our solar system. But this is neither his home nor his grave. For man, as created in the divine image, and thus ' partaking in the divine nature,' is in his essential being spirit. Man is involved in nature yet transcends it ; this is at once his grandeur and his tragedy; and the mystery of human life and death—the enigma which man is to himself—turns on that tension and duality.

This is the given fact of our experience—or at least of what our experience seems to be. If we are to make any sense of it at all it has got to be accounted for somehow, by the Christian interpretation, or by another. Secularism solves the enigma by the simple denial that it exists. All the facts cited by religion as pointing to man's spiritual nature and his commerce with trans-natural reality it dismisses outright as just illusory. There cannot be anything that is not nature. This ' everythingism ' as C. S. Lewis calls it, is no doubt a short and easy way with the Dissenter in natural man ; and it is, as he says, " congenial to our minds, because it is the natural philosophy of a totalitarian, mass-producing conscripted age." [1] But it is also at the same time an equally short and easy way with secularism. For if all our ' higher ' experience is illusory it follows that ' absolute values ' are illusory, and accordingly there is no absolute truth. Thus, like every other form of scepticism, secularist thought becomes committed to the strictly meaningless assertion which every undergraduate reading Greats inflicts on his tutor during his first term—the truth is that all truth is relative (*always provided* that *this* truth is absolute).

We are not likely to get very far on that line. On the other hand, most forms of Humanism sincerely and conscientiously attempt to do full justice to that in man which transcends the necessity of the natural order. But limited as they are, *ex hypothesi*, to the concept of a spiritual reality which is, in some sense, the creation of man himself, they cannot substantiate its validity. So like Shelley in Matthew Arnold's dictum (but actually, indeed, how unlike Shelley !) ' they beat their luminous wings in the void in vain.' Christianity claims to be a real faith for real people in a real world. The Church contends that the Christian doctrine can explain man to himself more effectively and offer a more convincing interpretation of the facts of human experience than any rival creed or philosophy. If so, people have every right to demand from it both positive insight into man's predicament in this actual world situation, and a Gospel that speaks to their condition. Some headings, at least, in the answer to that demand I have tried to suggest in the following paragraphs.

## (a) Man as Created.

The Biblical doctrine is a direct challenge to one of those uncriticised assumptions which the modern West takes for

[1] *Miracles*, p. 199.

granted. Man is a creature, not the lord of creation. The world belongs to God, not to man. On the question of public *versus* private ownership Christianity has not much to say; it is rather a technical than a moral issue. Its primary concern is to insist that all human ownership is relative because God is Sovereign and Owner of ' the round world and all that is therein '—(cf. Leviticus xxv. 23). It is not ours to do what we like with it. The lie in the soul of a scientific age is the idea that man can find salvation by increasing control of his environment, without reference to the will of the Creator. This comes to mean, in effect, exploiting nature for his own convenience or aggrandisement, and seeking to impose his own will upon it. Hence we get power divorced from morality and science devoid of ethical direction—culminating in the atom bomb. To-day we are within measurable distance of annihilating life on the whole planet. But man fulfils the law of his creaturehood only in obedience to the Creator's will. When that is defied or ignored man and his society come to ruin. We exploit the soil and it becomes a dust-bowl. True husbandmen know that it must be reverenced. *Naturae non imperatur nisi parendo.*

This sense of creaturely dependence on a Being, or beings, other than himself is a normal and unquestioned element in the religious experience of man at the agricultural stage of society. For there indeed it is constantly borne in upon him that his physical survival is bound up with the operation of forces which he did not make and cannot alter but must try to understand and obey.

It is probable that we have here the origin both of magic and of ' natural religion ' as well as the germ of scientific enquiry. It is taken for granted all through the Bible, where it is gradually enriched and clarified by the recognition that man's health and wealth depend on obedience to that law of righteousness which is wrought into the fabric of God's world. All this, of course, has been widely recognised outside the Biblical tradition—in the Stoic philosophy, to go no further —and is part of the content of ' natural law.' But the Bible gives it a characteristic emphasis through its knowledge of the ' Living God.'

Under the artificial conditions of an urbanised and industrial society, where men are removed from contact with the land, and live almost exclusively surrounded by man-made inventions and appliances, this sense of dependence upon God grows dim and may be even virtually eradicated, so that ' religion means nothing at all to me.' This, it may be held, is at the root of much of our social and spiritual sickness. Human life to-day is unnatural, not in the sense of being no longer primitive, but in that of being lived round a false centre and therefore pursuing radically false aims. It is no good exhorting men to be religious while the whole framework of their lives and the ends to which their activity is directed are thus so profoundly irreligious and violate the laws of man's being. A radical redirection is necessary— that is, in religious vocabulary, Conversion.

Man is a creature, but alone among creatures he has been entrusted by God with a delegated power of creation, to co-operate with the creative purpose. Made in the image of God the Creator, man expresses his nature in creating. He may do this in defiance of the Will—the Eden-saga follows the Creation-saga. But in so doing he betrays himself and disorganises his whole constitution. Slowly we must re-learn that lesson. It is those who live by raising the crops —the most obvious and exemplary instance of co-operation with the Creator—who still to-day can best understand the religious pattern and setting of human life. True though it may be that Christianity first took root in an urban civilisa-tion, it was not our kind of urban civilisation ; it was not insulated from the land.[1] It may perhaps be that our sick society can only be healed by a new Benedictine experiment. At any rate it is true that in the countryside the Church has now its best opportunity, both of social and of religious leadership. The country parish may yet prove to be the key to the reconversion of England.

[1] See footnote, p. 29.

And the new concern of the Church with agriculture may have far-reaching sociological consequences. For if we can once begin to rediscover the ' natural ' end of man's creative activity as co-operation with the will of God, that discovery can be carried out into the other departments of industry and the whole modern economic complex. The consequences would be revolutionary. Livelihood could again become vocation and work could be integrated with worship. For then we could see that the aim of all industry is the satisfaction of human need ' for God's glory and the relief of man's estate ' ; and that—in direct contradiction to the dominant assumption of our own time—production was made for man, not man for production.

For Christians, the ' end ' of the creative purpose as the will to the perfection of persons [1] is revealed, in principle, in the Incarnation. What its content may be in detail, under the ever-changing conditions of physical, social and economic environment, every generation has to enquire anew. The enquiry is now exceptionally difficult. But the exposition of Christian theology will have to be more and more closely related to these current sociological problems —i.e. to situations and circumstances which are not in themselves specifically ' religious.' " What is Man ? In what sense is his society a valid and necessary mode of life for his accomplishment of God's will ? What is his obligation to the natural resources which his ingenuity enables him to exploit ? What are the basic psychological needs of his nature in work and play ? " These are the sort of questions with which a living Church has now to deal, and theology must take hands with anthropology and sociology and psychology if answers are to be found for them.[2]

(b) *Man in his Environment*

As creature, man is involved in the order of nature, by which his whole experience is conditioned. ' First that which

---

[1] See below pp. 78 sq.
[2] M. Reckitt : *From Maurice to Temple*, ch. vii. para. 5.

is natural '; but never in this world can he knock down the ladder or disown the mother who gave birth to him. His total organisation is psycho-physical. Thus into his highest spiritual achievements he must carry his natural inheritance with all its necessities and its limitations, and all the past that has made him what he is. Most inevitably and decisively, he must carry the sentence of mortality. This is indeed the limiting condition by which man's situation is defined. The whole colour and texture of his experience, the traditions of organised society, the quality of all great art and literature, are pervaded by this fact of death. (' Mortal men, Hal, mortal men.') This from the first has been man's central problem and at least one magnificent civilisation has been constructed round preoccupation with it.

It needs no Christianity to remind us of our involvement in the natural order, though Christian piety sometimes forgets it, while Naturalism forgets everything else—or interprets ' nature ' too narrowly. The Biblical and Christian interpretation of man's natural origin and environment depends upon its understanding of nature from a God-centred point of view. Nature, as seen within a theistic world-view, is not self sufficient or self explanatory but is instrumental to spirit and organised by a spiritual purpose—the outward form of a sacramental universe. When, as in the ' scientific attitude,' nature is regarded as subsistent in its own right, then the resultant theory of man cannot but be limited to Naturalism and man is ' explained ' in terms of bio-chemistry, his endocrine glands or his conditioned reflexes. All these may be valid explanations of this or that mode of man's behaviour, but they certainly do not ' explain ' man. All these factors do, to an extent still undefined, affect temperament, mental dispositions and character ; but if no other factors were operative there could be no character to affect. Endocrine secretions may be healthy or unhealthy, but not good or bad.

But organic behaviour, at any level, is by way of response to environment. The emergence, in man, of spiritual capacities, whether aesthetic, rational or moral, is thus at least *a priori* evidence (which still requires to be tested and verified) of spiritual reality in the Universe. And if the Christian world-view is true, the environment to which man responds and within which his life is framed, is at once natural and supra-natural. It is not now one and now the other, it is both at once, always and everywhere. Only if that is true can we account for the characteristic facts of human experience, alike in its failures and in its victories. But it entails that man's life as spirit never is and never can be lived on an exclusively ' spiritual ' level. Christianity is more than ' religion.' Human life is all of one piece. Our need for bread, our need for one another and our need for God are all interdependent—as the Church affirms in its Eucharist.

It follows accordingly that for Christian thought the status and vocation of man are to be attributed not to pure spirit but to man within the ' orders of creation '—family, race, cultural inheritance, civic responsibilities and so forth. Religious man apart from these contexts is as much of a fiction as economic man.[1] In one sense, no doubt, these ' accidental ' contexts are irrelevant to the Christian judgement. " In Christ there can be neither Jew nor Greek, man nor woman, slave or free." What that means is that Christ died for all and that all are of equal worth in the sight of God. Neither the colour of a man's face nor his rank nor his financial circumstances can affect his standing before God or his position in the Christian Church. " At the point at which alone man has true dignity he is completely equal to all his fellow-men ; this infinite value is of such a kind as to shut out all superiority." [2] But it does not mean that physical endowment, sex, parentage, occupational skill, nationality or the other facts in a human situation which are

---

[1] " When one strips man of all his functions as a member of a race, people, party, family or corporation, one reduces the very province of personality ; for personality emerges not by rejection of social ties, but by their more complete assimilation and incarnation. The unfettered individual was less of a man than the man of the middle ages "—Mumford : *op. cit.*, p. 253.

[2] Temple : *The Church Looks Forward*, p. 81.

just ' given,' are irrelevant to our Christian vocation. They
are the divinely appointed material through which and within
which it must be realised. We must ' do our duty in that
state of life into which it shall please God to call us '—after
all, there is nowhere else to do it. (The common misquota-
tion, 'it hath pleased God' seems to give sanction to a caste-
society in which the attempt to ' better oneself ' is wrong ;
but that is not what the Catechism says.) Therefore these
given factors in our environment—whether our bodies or
our national history—come within the sphere of religious
insight and pertain to the ' calling of a Christian man.'

It would seem to follow that Christian theology must be
ready to devote far more attention to those environmental
conditions which are the setting for man's task on earth.
Because we reject historical determinism we must not ignore
the element of truth in the economic interpretation of history.
For we are not nearly so ' free ' as we like to think. It is in
fact a strictly limited area within which real freedom of
choice is open to us. We did not choose to come into the
world at all, nor shall we decide when we are to leave it. It
is not we who laid down the rules by which the game of life
must be played in the threescore years that we have here
for learning it. These limitations govern the life of man and
neither our piety nor our wit can alter them.

But we are not, therefore, slaves of circumstance. There
are no inevitabilities in history. There are many inevitable
things that have never happened. Because he is spirit man
is not confined to any determined pattern of response ; so
that there is real indeterminacy. Faith, courage and imagination can not merely ' rise above circumstances ' but can
change the whole direction of events. What I want to stress
is simply that freedom is freedom within a conditioning
environment and is never, therefore, absolute or unqualified.
Moral choices are not made in a vacuum. Good motives and
' goodwill ' are not enough ; we have to deal with concrete
situations in which very often we must be content to do
what we *can*, not what we should choose to do if the situation

were other than it is. The Christian must seek to discover
the will of God not away from these limitations but inside
them. And, as sin is part of our environment, it may often
be that the only choice open is not that between good and
evil, but that between a greater evil and a lesser. Where
this is so, the ' lesser of two evils ' is not only the morally
right choice, but in a relative and sinful world it is our
Christian duty before God.

To many Christians this may sound a hard saying. It
may seem to be too much tainted with ' compromise.' But
that criticism would miss the real point. There can be for
Christians only one standard of moral loyalty and obligation
and that ' ideal ' is never to be compromised. The real
difficulty and the real challenge of Christian conduct in this
actual world is to know how this categorical imperative can
be obeyed and expressed in action in the particular complex
of circumstances, which may be singularly un-ideal. In the
world into which we seem to be now moving this point will
become more and more important. For Christians will get
nothing done at all if they are afraid of making their hands
dirty. They must either act or go underground. We may
yet be driven ' back to the catacombs,' but to go there
voluntarily is defeatism. We must not digress further down
this path, though what I have tried to suggest in these three
paragraphs has a direct bearing on what follows.

If the world belongs to the Living God, there cannot
be anything in our environment which is unrelated to his
righteous purpose, and even that which is definitely evil
depends for its existence on his goodness. There are many
forces in operation in long-term historical developments of
which we have yet so little understanding that they seem to
*us* to be merely ' blind ' determinisms. They just take
charge, as it seems to us, of history, quite independently of
all human purpose ; yet the survival of the human race and
the fulfilment of man's task on earth seems, under God, to
be bound up with them. Of these, at the moment, one of the
most challenging is that of the ebb and flow of population,

about which at present we know far too little.  Yet here we
encounter an elemental force which can bring all our hopes
and plans to ruin ;  and civilisation might be overwhelmed
by the pressure of population on food-supply.  What conditions, physical or mental, are favourable or adverse to
fertility ?  Moral factors are certainly involved, but these by
themselves will not solve the problems.  Again, mysterious
subterranean forces break forth from time to time out of the
depths of the collective consciousness which turn on civilisation to destroy it.  How and to what extent are these related
to facts which are, or could be brought, under man's control ?
What social or occupational conditions make for psychological
stability, which tend to create discontent and violence ?  In
these borderlands between ethics and the sciences Christian
research is imperatively needed.

These and similar investigations must obviously enough
bear directly on the causes of war and its elimination.  We
cannot doubt that this latter is God's will for us.  But it is
certain that it cannot be done by religious and ' spiritual '
means alone, or by appeal to a moral authority which the
mass of mankind are not willing to acknowledge.  And what
this means in effect is that the Church can no longer hold
itself aloof from immediate, practicable alleviations—however
far short of ' Christian ' ideals—which may indeed be inspired
by Christian loyalties but have to be carried out by other
agencies.[1]  In so far as they are carried out by politics and
governmental agencies it must be by those methods which
are proper to them—by diplomacy, by trade-agreements, by
law and in the last resort, by armaments.  Because they
know a ' more excellent way ' Christians are not thereby
given neutral rights towards other attempts on a less-than-
Christian level aimed at the enhancement of human welfare.
These belong to their Christian vocation, since man as a
spiritual being is yet involved in nature and history.  Moreover while it is true, by the grace of God, that ' a man can be

[1] On all this, see A. D. Lindsay : *The Two Moralities*.  Eyre and Spottis-
woode,

a Christian in any circumstances,' the full Christian life
cannot be lived nor is a Christian civilisation possible except
in a certain ordering of society which the Church by itself
can no longer bring about.

It certainly looks as though, more and more, the Christian
conscience will have to come to terms with a rather violently
new approach to the implications of Christian action in the
mixed civilisation of our time ; and it will involve many
torturing questions.  For the Church was the pioneer in
education and the social services simply in Christ's name
and for love of souls.  A very great deal of what the Church
initiated has been and will be increasingly taken over by
the State or by municipal authorities.  What should be its
attitude towards these ?  Is it to write them off as merely
secular ?  If not, on what terms can it collaborate ?  The
problem arises not only in this country but also all over the
Christian mission fields, not least in regard to the far-reaching
schemes of the new African ground-nuts corporation, where
at every turn politico-economic issues will interlock with
moral and religious.  If the Church is not to fail the people
for whom it is answerable to its Lord, it will (as it seems)
have to do its work through organisations which are in some
sense alien from it.  And this will entail heart-searching
difficulties.

Moreover, it can no longer be maintained that forms of
political government are irrelevant to the nature of man and
the Christian understanding of it.  The day is past when we
could glibly say that whatever is best administered is best, and
that with a sufficiency of 'goodwill' any form of government
can be Christianised.  As things are now, this is just not true.
Some political regimes are incompatible with human rights
and the dignity of man.  About these Christians cannot
profess neutrality.  In the bitter and cruel world that lies
before us they will have to take politics very much more
seriously, and may have to think deeply about the hard
saying, " I came not to bring peace but rather division."  In
future they will have to take sides on political questions,

and often different sides ; and, in the last dreadful extremity, may have to take station at the barricades.

" Man goeth forth to his work and to his labour : until the evening." That was part of the evidence, for the Psalmist, of the activity of the Living God in the world of nature and in the lives of men. Man's intercourse with his environment under the Providence of the Creator, in the day by day ' secular ' activities through which the life of humanity is sustained, is thus invested with religious sanction. It is part of the hallowing of God's name. It is part of man's due to his Creator. According to the insight of the Bible, he starts on his career with the divine blessing on the skill of his mind and the labour of his hands. " God *blessed* man and said Be fruitful and multiply and replenish the earth and subdue it." These mundane labours and preoccupations are not, as is too frequently suggested, alternatives to the requirements of religion. They are within the purpose of God for man. In earning his bread and bringing up a family, in the exercise of his powers of mind and body and in the finding out of many inventions, a man may truly be doing God service. " These maintain the fabric of the world " (Eccles. xxxviii. 34), and it is a shockingly irreligious attitude which denies Christian significance to all this. There are many things in life which are not ' religious ' but none which are not under God's sovereignty and not to be approached in a religious spirit.

At the cost, it may be, of one-sided emphasis, I have deliberately been underlining some facts, inherent in man's situation, which Christians on their side tend to overlook or to find unwelcome and unpalatable. But obviously these are not the only facts, nor is this all that is to be said about them. If it were, there could be no Christianity. They are elements in a richer whole from which they derive their meaning and validity. If nothing in man is ever purely spiritual, neither is anything in him ' merely ' natural. Since

the Renaissance, European thought has been vitiated by a
fatal dualism between ' natural ' and ' supernatural,' and
when the supernatural is excluded, the natural pattern of
life falls to pieces.  Secular life is corrupted by worldliness,
while religion tends to degenerate into pietism.  (Neither the
Yogi nor the Kommissar could be representative figures in
a Christian culture.)

Accordingly, it must also be affirmed with no less and
indeed with even stronger emphasis, that no attempted
adjustment to environment on a purely physical or instinctive
level corresponds to the facts of human nature, or will be
able to satisfy man's needs.  A naturalistic theory of human
life is not merely blind to certain ' higher ' facts, it falsifies
and misreads all the facts.  That ' man shall not live by
bread alone ' is not a piece of idealistic uplift, it is an entirely
realistic statement.  We have learnt once more through the
discipline of experience that if we try to live by bread alone
we cannot even supply ourselves with bread.[1]  The biological
instincts and impulses belong to the nature of man as God has
made him (' Male and female created he them ').  And it
may be a legitimate indictment against modern industrial
civilisation that some of these instinctive ' vitalities ' are
denied their outlet and satisfaction, with injurious psychological results.  But there is a far more serious indictment—
that in a deeply secularised society they are denied human
satisfaction because the awareness of God is blotted out, and
with it the true ends of human striving.  For the instincts
are the instincts of man, with his rational and moral consciousness ;  and if they are not moralised and sublimated
they are, as it were, turned back on themselves, and men
become listless, unstable and disharmonised.  To a far
greater extent than can be calculated the frustration of
contemporary society may be due, in the end, to this under-

[1] Cf. " Only those who are aware of the importance of man's higher needs
will be capable of even providing intelligently for bare food and shelter "—
Mumford : *op. cit.*, p. 415.

lying cause. Jung has committed himself to the statement (which could, in all probability, be corroborated in almost any medical consulting-room) that a high percentage of all his patients are people who have been driven to seek treatment because their religious consciousness has been atrophied. We are only now beginning to understand that the neglect or repression of religion may be, not only impious or regrettable, but actually dangerous and destructive, because it does violence to human nature.

The most evident illustration of all these facts is to be found in the breakdown of the family, the meeting-point of the natural and spiritual. There are no doubt many contributory causes—physical, economic and psychological—and it is more important to deal constructively with matters like housing and family allowances than to pass resolutions in Church assemblies ' deploring ' the frightful statistics of divorce. Nor can we have anything but welcome for the recommendations of Mr. Justice Denning. But the central core of the problem *is* religious—the elimination of spiritual reality from the contemporary Western mind. The only truly effective ' marriage guidance ' would be the recovery of faith in God. There can be no restoration of family-life nor any rebuilding of genuine community till it is seen that ' natural ' human groups come to themselves and attain their true ends only by virtue of participation in transnatural and spiritual realities—in ' one great city of gods and men,' or, as Christians say, the community of the Holy Spirit.

#### (c) Man as Rational.

*Homo sapiens* is his definition, and man without some light of reason, however rudimentary, would be sub-man. It is man's prerogative of reason which enables him to rise above nature and lifts him out of the realm of necessity by calculated response to his environment, thus winning his primacy over earthly creatures. By it he can learn nature's secrets and become inventor, scientist and philosopher. All who have meditated on human life have found in man's rational endowment the most distinctively human of his attributes and that in him which is ' nearest to divinity.' " How noble in reason ! How infinite in faculty (invention) ! In apprehension how like a God ! " And in this glorification of reason Humanists and Christians join hands. Christianity by its doctrine of the Logos claims to be ' speaking a rational language ' and is pledged to the rationality of the universe, which is reflected in man's reasoning mind. (The attempt made by some Christian theologians, both in medieval and modern times, to throw doubt on the validity of reason as an instrument by which we can know God, undermines the whole basis of theology.) This is indeed the justification of Humanism, at least in its more philosophical varieties. Here Christianity and Humanism are able to walk in the house of God as friends. And here in passing it may be pointed out that the Wisdom-literature of the Bible, as the meeting-point of the Greek and the Hebrew insights, becomes increasingly relevant to our own age.

There are, however, certain considerations to which both parties, from their different standpoints, may rightly be urged to devote closer thought.

(1) It is implied in the doctrine of the Logos that all creative exercise of reason in art, science, philosophy and so forth is a partaking in the divine Word, who is the true light that lighteth every man. It follows that intellectual integrity and the fullest and freest activity of the mind is not only a true part of man's vocation, but also an element in Christian worship. This marriage of science with religion is one of the greatest needs of the world to-day. It has been one of the weaknesses of the Church that it has too long been content to stand intellectually on the defensive, whereas it should be the pioneer thinker, proving its power to out-think secular culture. It has been said that Marxians and Humanists are asking the right questions but giving false answers, while Christians, who know the true answers, have not yet learnt to ask the right questions.[1] Yet religious people on their

[1] *The Student Movement*, March 1948, pp. 1–3.

side must recognise that the dedicated artist or scientist,
though he may prefer to call himself an atheist or may reach
conclusions which seem to be irreligious, may nevertheless
be worshipping the true God.

(2) On the other hand, Humanists may be reminded that
reason in man is not self-sufficient. Like all our endowments
and capacities it is ever pointing out beyond itself to a
' farther shore ' on the other side of the frontier. Reason
makes a *claim* on the universe ; and this is met, according
to Christian theism, by the self-communication of the Living
God, both to the created world as rational and to the reasoning mind which can apprehend it. When thought lacks this
theistic background reason can claim no ultimate validity,
and thinking tends to breakdown into scepticism. Now it is
an extremely striking fact that the ' flight from reason '
(which we have already noticed as characteristic of the last
half century), did not originate among the masses. It was
initiated by ' intellectuals.' Indeed it is hardly too much to
say that the main stream of intellectual output, whether
aesthetic, speculative or moral, has been tainted and corrupted
by scepticism. And it must surely be more than a coincidence
that this movement of sceptical intellectualism seems to have
gathered force, *pari passu*, with the decline of Christian faith
and practice.

In recent years scientists and philosophers have been
engaged, by a paradoxical effort, in blowing the bridges for
their own traffic and cutting their own lines of communication. There are well-known scientific writers who have cast
radical doubts on their own premises. Indeed they have
gone out of their way to insist that the sciences can tell us
nothing about the constitution of the universe. All they
can do is to record pointer-readings ; to log the observed
recurrence of sequences, tabulated in algebraic equations ; to
indicate in mathematical formulae the behaviour of hypothetical existences. What these are in themselves they
cannot tell us, nor what are the laws, if any, which control
them. It has even been said that the formulæ would hold

good if the physical universe were not there at all.[1]   If we
find evidence of rationality in the universe which the sciences
investigate, it is probably read into it by our own minds.

So, by a queer turning of the wheel, science, which had
demanded for itself the right to prescribe the laws for all
thought, which must conform to the scientific pattern or
forfeit its title to respectability, seems now to be heading
towards total scepticism.   (Unguarded theologians have been
too ready to make religious capital out of this trend.   But
to believe in a ' God in the gaps ' which are left by scientific
agnosticism is at best a highly precarious form of Theism.)
If we ask what has led to this scientific scepticism, we shall
certainly find contributory causes in the researches of the
new physics in the field of radio-activity.   Here the evidence
seems to suggest a principle of contingency and indetermina-
tion in the behaviour of the atomic structure.   And this has
involved a drastic revision of previous conceptions of causality
and indeed of the whole idea of ' law ' in nature.   But this
may not be in itself the chief, as it is certainly not the sole,
ground for it.   It is to be noted, for our present purposes, that
the sciences had been becoming philosophies, and inadequate
philosophies at that, because they were tied to the axioms of
Naturalism.   Those axioms have broken down and with them
the metaphysics of the scientists.

" It was (says Whitehead) a notable event in the history
of ideas, when the clergy of the Western races began to waver
in their appeal to constructive reason.   More recently
scientists and critical philosophers have followed the Methodist
example." [2]   For philosophers, too, have been indulging in a
radical and far-reaching scepticism ;  and once that serpent
of fundamental doubt has been let loose in the academic
garden, what is there left for philosophy to do ?   It can no

---

[1] It is remarked in a masterly review of Bertrand Russell's *History of
Western Philosophy*, that the " mathematical sciences are not mere games
with symbols but refer to fact ;  the attempt to amputate the final reference
to fact is an aspect of the modern retreat from reality "—*Times Lit. Supp.*,
December 1946.

[2] *Adventures of Ideas*, pp. 27–28.

longer discharge its proper functions, for it has repudiated its own axioms. In our time, as in the late medieval period, the enormous amount of new empirical data was bound to have a disruptive effect. In particular it was bound to prove fatal to nineteenth-century Absolute Idealism, which can never admit an evolving universe to the status of full metaphysical reality. For, if time belongs to the nature of things, ' static ' concepts are no longer applicable. But ' Nominalism,' in all its modern varieties of scepticism about universals, and the objectivity of real relations, cannot but end in an intellectual *cul de sac*. It can take refuge in Logical Positivism—but Positivism, having ruled out all knowledge that is not empirical, can have no room for any logic that is more than formal. Or, in despair of knowing a real world, it can confine itself to epistemology and enquire what is the meaning of meaning. But no theory of knowledge, however much it may wish to, can in fact stop short of metaphysics. Knowledge, after all, is knowledge of something, and cannot be discussed in abstraction from the nature and quality of what is known. As an empty form it cannot exist at all.

Failure to recognise this was responsible for what has been called ' the Cartesian faux pas.' [1] Descartes started out from a fallacy. For nobody can be ever just thinking—he must be always thinking about something. Descartes assumed that the one certain truth was his own existence as a thinking subject, and proceeded to ask what he could deduce from that about the reality of the world outside him. But in the very act of saying ' I think,' he was really implicating his mind with the whole known and knowable Universe.[2] What he ought to have begun by saying was, ' I am part of a total universe, thinking about it and what is in it.' Unless there was something else that he knew to start

---

[1] Temple: *Nature, Man and God*, pp. 57–82.

[2] " *Cogito ergo sum* proves nothing about the existence of a thinking individual . . . but it does point to the indubitable existence of human society : the words as such indicate the existence of other selves and imply the entire history of the human race "—Mumford : *op. cit.*, p. 254 ; also Maritain's recent study.

with, he could have had no cogitations. We know our minds
as subjects of knowledge because we first know something
else ; and, in the end, the reality of God is the presupposition
of all rational thought.

Behind all this drift towards scepticism is that false
conception of Reason, by which it becomes identified with
Rationalism. It is I who think, not my reason as a separable
faculty of the mind. Thought engages the whole personality,
and it was a fatally false development when rationality came
to be equated simply with intellectual self-consistency. As
the rationality of the Universe is revealed also in its moral
structure, so reason is manifest in conscience, in the appreciation of beauty, and in the recognition of other persons.
' Wisdom ' in the Bible has a moral content and is never mere
intellectualism ; it means the right ordering of life and
therefore the fear of the Lord is its beginning.[1] What
completely justifies itself to reason is the evidence of intelligible purpose, and therefore the fullest exercise of reason,
as the activity of the whole man, is the knowledge and fear of
the Lord. Man without the knowledge of God is not man.
" Faith in human reason," says Professor Hodgson, " is a
corollary of faith in God, if we believe in the God of the
biblical revelation. Nor, if we accept this revelation can we
regard this reason as so corrupted by sin as to be wholly
unreliable, for God is revealed to us as appealing to it (by
the message of the prophets). . . . According to the Bible,
the divine redemptive activity begins with God's endorse-
ment of natural theology." [2] But intellectual emancipation,
which belongs to our God-given task as men, tends to moral
and intellectual nihilism if it is the work of the critical
intelligence unrelated to its religious context.

And reason itself stands in need of redemption. For it
is not so free and independent as rationalists and humanists
have believed. It may be distorted by subconscious bias, it

---

[1] Herbert Spencer " was a man who seemed not to understand the difference
between living reasonably and living by reason "—Gerald Bullett : *George
Eliot*, p. 237.

[2] *Towards a Christian Philosophy*, p. 141.

may be obscured by defects of character (" if the light that is within thee be darkness, how great is that darkness ! "). Our most seemingly impartial judgements may be conditioned by social environment, economic self-interest, frustrated instinct and many other non-rational influences. Marx and Freud may have recalled attention to what is implied in the Augustinian doctrine that reason has been corrupted by the fall of man. We need not take this to exaggerated extremes— as Professor Hodgson's statement above reminds us. But neither can it be airily dismissed. Rationalists are too much at ease in Zion. There can be no such thing as ' unaided ' reason—an idea which is meaningless for Christian thought ; and reason can only become fully reasonable [1] when delivered from its inherent limitations—when cleansed and illuminated by spirit.[2]

### (d) Man as Child of God.

Organic life supervenes upon inorganic and thereby modifies its ' behaviour '—its chemical reactions and so forth. Consciousness grows within organic life, and develops into self-conscious mind which invests organic and instinctive behaviour with new capacities and characteristics. All the needs and endowments of man are thus throughout transfigured and transvalued by the dominant fact that he is, at least potentially, a child of God and heir of eternal life. His biological, social and rational nature all take on, as it were, a different colour and require more than ' natural ' satisfaction because man is created in God's image.

" God created man in His own image." It may be said that all the rest of the Bible is a commentary on that phrase, which is the presupposition of the Gospel. To discuss it in detail would require a volume. We take it here to cover the implications of moral and spiritual personality, which it ascribes to the gift of the Living God. Man is formed of the

---

[1] Reasonable service in Romans xii. 1 is translated ' spiritual ' in R.V. margin.

[2] See Alan Richardson : *Christian Apologetics*, ch. iii. (The idea of natural reason in St. Thomas rests on " an unduly optimistic estimate.")

dust of the earth by the age-long evolutionary process ; like
Adam in the Sistine mural he is summoned into being as
man, in his unique and distinctively human character, by
the touch of the Living God upon him. In other words,
man becomes a ' self,' a subject, a centre of moral experience,
in response to God's self-communication to him.

Humanist insights carry us to the point at which, unless
Christianity is true, Humanism itself becomes illusory. The
possibility of self-knowledge and of conscience, which is
essentially self-critical, presupposes that there is a ' true
self '—inchoate it may be, but already real—which transcends the empirical consciousness. Again, man transcends
the temporal process by which his whole experience is conditioned ; otherwise there could be no awareness of the
passage of time, of ' before ' and ' after,' or of the transitori-
ness of life and of even our deepest and highest satisfactions.
This mysterious fact of self-transcendence, which is the
essential quality of spirit, reaches out beyond ' natural '
frontiers towards a goal in some order of reality which is not
confined within space-time dimensions.

If all this experience is delusory, if there is not in the
nature of things itself some real foothold for personality,
some response to this insistent claim, then the whole life of
man is a mistake and nothing in his experience makes sense.
If man is indeed the ' last word ' in the universe, he is alone,
friendless and unsupported in a vast impersonal process by
which at last he must be overwhelmed. Only within a
Theistic world-view can personal life find any true validity.
Ours is the religion of personality in a sense which can be
claimed by no other. The Living God of the Bible and
Christianity is the God to whom persons are dear. Personal
life come to its fulfilment in the personal ' encounter ' with
God which constitutes responsible self-hood.

If man is created in the divine image then he is fundamentally good. (The de-nigration of man which is now fashion-
able might seem to be rather in character with Diogenes than
with spokesmen of the Gospel of God.) *Whose* is this image

and superscription ? If it is that of the Father of Spirits, then the whole story holds together. To be man is to be capable of God—of receiving that which is ever being offered to him. In every recognition of good he is responding to the divine initiative, in all appreciation of beauty, in every choice between right and wrong he is confronted by the Living God and the Living God moves towards man. Personal life in all its implications is the self-revelation of God to man and in him ; and all this is fulfilled and guaranteed by the Incarnation, which is ' God's Yes.' (2 Cor. ii. 21.)

Christianity ' discovered' the individual—disengaging him, as it were, from the collective ; but it was the individual, not in the modern sense of unethical and anarchic individualism, but in his responsibility before God. Men are real, man is an abstraction. But it is equally to be borne in mind that personality is in its nature social and can only be realised in community. The disorganisation of personal life to-day and the disintegration of community are intimately and causally related.

If personal life, in its full meaning, consists in communion with the Living God, it exists in the eternal dimension. (' He is not the God of the dead but of the living.') The virtual fading-out of this dimension from the contemporary Western consciousness, and indeed very largely from the Christian consciousness, impoverishes life to a degree which it is hardly possible to exaggerate. The abdication of moral responsibility, the apathy, the frustration and despair and that ' lack of incentive ' of which so much is heard, are all results of this lost conviction. Within a three-dimensional frame of existence life seems to be devoid of meaning. Nothing indeed matters more to-day whether for Christianity or for the world than that the Church should once again recapture the true notes of an other-worldly faith. Nothing would do more to restore vitality to the life of the Church as well as to secular culture.[1]

Moreover belief in man's eternal destiny must profoundly and radically influence Christian political and social thinking.

[1] See more fully below, ch. v.

Loss of faith in God and life eternal is one of the tap-roots of totalitarianism.  If man is but a creature of time, drowned in the relativities of history, then it is very hard to resist the argument that the State matters more than its citizens ;  it is not ' eternal ' but it endures much longer, and can enfold far more stable values than the brief years of the fleeting individual.  But if man is heir to everlasting life, then it is men and women who endure, while the State (and the ' undying race ') are transitory, and the State exists for men—not men for it.  All this line of thought has an urgent relevance to the central political question of our time.  If the Christian doctrine of man is true, the State has its place in the providential order, and its end and justification are moral—to provide those conditions for the good life within which men and women can prepare themselves for the fulfilment of eternal destinies.  On that rests its claim to our allegiance. If a secular doctrine comes to hold the field, the new-model state will too soon degenerate into something little more than ' big-scale piracy.' [1]  Thus the Christian conviction of eternal life is the most effective bulwark of liberty.  No other defences are comparable with it.

Man's creation in the image of God is the basis of any valid claim to freedom, education, opportunity, the right to be treated as an end in himself, or to any other charter of human rights.  These rights are not intrinsic to man.  His status and value are conferred upon him by the gracious will of God towards him.  His worth is his value in the sight of God (Luke xii. 24).  Apart from that, man is ' that which is not ' (1 Cor. i. 28).  The ' sacredness of human personality,' the respect for human dignities and decencies, which lie at the base of a Christian civilisation, depend on nothing innate in man, nor upon any concession by the State, but upon a divine endowment and prerogative which no earthly power gave nor can take away.  The classical Christian theory of the State, as worked out by the medieval theologians, rests on that fundamental axiom.  It requires emphatic re-affirmation.

[1] St. Augustine's *Magna latrocinia.*

## CHAPTER IV

## GOOD NEWS FOR MAN

IT has become almost common form to declare that civilisation has no future except on the basis of ' Christian principles.' It is also, at long last, being more clearly recognised that we cannot hope to retain ' Christian standards,' apart from belief in the Christian world-view. The illusion that Christian ethics were secure and a permanent element in Western culture independently of the religion which sustained them is now revealed as an insubstantial mirage. And just there is the failure of non-Christian Humanism. What a Christian civilisation has hitherto meant has been one which accepted common beliefs, about God and the world and human destiny, and acknowledged common standards of moral authority—however much these were denied in practice. We have, as it were, sold out the capital, but imagined that we could still draw the income from it. Dr. John Baillie speaks of " a generation—in many ways a noble generation— which desperately desired to call a halt *at that point* to a dissipation of the Christian outlook which up to that point they had done everything in their power to encourage. What can be the basis of any faith in ideals of any kind except a ' belief about *reality* ? ' And if it is to be called in to support *Christian* ideals how can it be expected to play its part effectively unless it be a Christian belief about reality ? " [1]

If we want to see in our time a revival of reverence for reason and the moral law, and respect for the dignity of man —and unless we do in fact witness that there will not be

[1] John Baillie : *What is Christian Civilisation ?* Christophers, pp. 48–49.

anything else left to see—that involves, as I have been arguing, a re-education into the Christian world-view. A radical change of mind may be required before the West can again believe the good news (Mk. i. 14). In the previous chapters we have examined some of the links in the interacting chain of cultural and intellectual causes in the drift away from the Christian outlook, and have marked some of the primary objectives in the consequential strategy of recovery.

And if it were true that knowledge is virtue, it might be comparatively straightforward going. But unfortunately it is not, and the crucial obstacle still defies our capture. Not only has civilisation gone astray in its thinking and its avowed social aims ; it has also rejected and disobeyed the law of God and his revealed purpose, both for societies and for individuals—" holding down the truth in unrighteousness " (Rom. i. 18). Thinking people are perfectly well aware of it. That knowledge is driven in upon our minds by the headlines in every morning's paper. We know that when we forsake the Lord our God and follow after the vain gods of the heathen, then " all these evils come upon us." We are set " between the blessing and the curse," like the people on the frontiers of the promised land, " between life and good or death and evil." " Therefore choose life, that thou mayest live " (Deut. xxx. 15–20). It is self-evident ; but we do not act on it. For despite our posturing and our braggadocio, men are not captains of their souls. There is no secure hope of man's recovery unless there is available to man a Power that can deliver us from evil, and a goodness that can make sinners whole. Neither intellectual conversion nor the most enlightened social architecture can avail to redeem men from sin.

All our miseries and our frustrations spring from that bitter root—and who can cure it ? For it was a vain dream that it could be extirpated by improved material standards and environment, or by any manipulation of externals or shifting of the balance of power, whether political or economic. Men are not less selfish or unscrupulous because wealth is being redistributed and new avenues opened to place and influence. The revolutions have not produced, as was predicted, a classless society, but a different and more ruthless class-warfare, and a new, but more cynical, privilege of caste. There is nothing to show that leftist regimes are more peace-loving or more law-abiding or less ' imperialistic ' than their predecessors—the evidence points in the opposite direction. Nor, because we know so much more than our fathers, have we gained any deeper illumination, spiritual humility and reverence, or responsibility in the use of knowledge. Too much of our elaborate education has apparently, like the Roman ' rhetoric,' been teaching people how to be clever and to 'get on' but not teaching them to be good. Not all the new apparatus of living or the things that we have can change what we are. No historical ' progress ' alters that. Men are sinners as they always have been ; and nothing could be good news for man in any profound and realistic sense which does not tell of deliverance from *that* bondage. No promise that falls short of that is taking the fundamental problem seriously.

According to the Christian understanding, man is neither an unfinished god nor a beast still but half-domesticated ; he is a spirit created by God in the divine image—but ' fallen.' Christian insight here is unaffected by the changed approach to the story of the ' Fall,' which is now commonly accepted as being not the account of an event which had occurred at the dawn of history but rather the mythological presentation of a permanent fact in our moral experience. (The notion of a ' premundane ' fall which has had an attraction for some distinguished thinkers, both in ancient times and in modern, is little more than a variant mythology ; for if taken strictly it contradicts itself. There cannot be any event outside the time-process.) Sin is man's melancholy privilege, not a hangover from sub-human ancestry, but a sign of his moral and spiritual endowment—a possibility always inherent in his very nature as spirit. An animal can, presumably, make a false choice, can (as the Greeks put it) miss the mark—even though that has no *ethical* significance ; and the evolution of species makes plain how disastrous may be the consequences. But only a child of God can commit sin.  Thus it is, by a resounding moral paradox, that the very fact of man's fallen state—his shame, his treachery and his humiliation—is evidence of his divine origin and therefore contains the pledge of his restoration.[1]  This does not minimise its gravity, but it does set the problem in its true perspective.  It sets it within the framework of redemption, where it can be regarded from the standpoint which must be the centre of all Christian thinking—not the failure of man but the victory of God.

The story of the Garden of Eden, as N. P. Williams showed in his Bampton lectures,[2] played little part in later Biblical thought, and it is never referred to in the Gospels. It may, or may not, have been a calamity for the developed theology of Christendom that St. Paul and St. Augustine built so much on it.  Certainly the thought, and the preaching, of the Western Church have sometimes been in danger of regarding man's depravity and corruption as the fundamental axioms of Theology.  That is at once unscriptural and sub-Christian.  The Bible holds that man is made in God's image, existing solely in virtue of his goodness, and sees his whole record in the light of Christ.[3]  And the core of the Gospel is the goodness of God and ' grace abounding to the chief of sinners.'  Nevertheless, the myth of Adam and Eve does in truth go to the heart of the matter by laying stress on man's first *disobedience*—self-assertion against the will of God (i.e., ' Pride ') as the root of all sin.  Moreover, it is more hopeful and more merciful and, it may be fairly claimed, more masculine than the Hellenistic and oriental theories, which attribute the origin of evil to the principle of individuality—the soul's descent from the realm of pure essence into

[1] Cf. " Thou (the woman) shalt bruise his (the serpent's) head, but he shall bruise thy heel."  Gen. iii. 4.

[2] *The Ideals of the Fall and of Original Sin.*

[3] Cf. the impressive extracts from F. D. Maurice on this point, collected by A. R. Vidler in *Witness to the Light.*  Scribners, New York, pp. 30 ff.

the world of matter and becoming. For if that is so ' original sin ' consists in the fact of our having been born, and that is radical, suicidal pessimism. On that showing we are damned into the world, and the historical process is damnation from which salvation is only to be found by the eradication of desire and the suppression of the will to live—i.e., by ceasing to be men and women. Christianity never said anything so ghastly.[1]

Christian thought is, in general, less concerned to speculate how evil ' got there ' than to proclaim how it may be cast out. Its interest lies in the practical solution rather than in theoretical speculation. But it does hold firmly that the seat of evil resides in no metaphysical necessity, but in the will of man as moral person. As moral person he is made in God's image. Thus goodness is ' prior ' to the evil and indeed the pre-condition of its existence ; even while he sins man is in God's hands, like a rebellious child in its mother's arms, and the image of God is never completely lost. Thus the Christian doctrine of the ' fall ' is fundamentally a hopeful doctrine.

The meaning of sin (as distinguished from ' sins ') is, as William Temple taught, self-centredness. It is the claim to false independence on the part of finite and created spirit, thinking and acting from the self as centre, not from the true centre of Reality, and therefore perenially involved in egoism, manifesting itself as the will-to-power. How this tends to pervert all man's activities (and not least virulently his religion) has been searchingly worked out by Reinhold Niebuhr in *The Nature and Destiny of Man*.[2] Human life is thereby disorganised, alienated from its true purpose and contradicting the law of its nature. There is ' a law of sin in our members,' in contradiction to the law of God. The

---

[1] How far that obsession with sex which has been the ' King Charles' Head ' in the Augustinian tradition has been due to infiltration from that camp, a book on this scale cannot stop to enquire. It is, however, important to remember that the Fall story finds the root-sin not in ' Concupiscence ' but in ' Pride.'

[2] Vol. 1. ch. vii–ix.

way of salvation is the movement out from the prison-house of the self-centred life to the service of God which is perfect freedom. But we cannot ourselves initiate that movement just because we are fatally inhibited by that very self-centredness which locks the door on us. The Gospel tells what the Living God has done, and is doing, to deliver us. "When he took man upon him to deliver him, he did not shrink from the womb of the Virgin."

The Gospel is Good News for man because it is a Gospel about God. First and last, the concern of Christianity is with the reality of the Living God—the Kingdom and the Power and the Glory—as the ground and meaning of the universe. The goodness of God is Creation's final law—goodness creating, hallowing and redeeming and, through all, regnant in majesty. But the course of history and the life of man had gone astray from the purpose of goodness and cannot be reconciled to moral reality by any immanent powers of its own or by any process of gradual improvement. The initiative must come from the source of goodness. Man's ultimate need is that which man cannot satisfy. Because we are sinners we cannot redeem ourselves. It is the Living God who is the Reconciler, and the Gospel declares that " God was in Christ reconciling the world unto himself " (II Cor. v. 19). Since that which is to be reconciled is sinful, it can be achieved only at the cost of suffering, which the goodness of God himself bears, undefeated.

This is the Christian doctrine of Atonement, so often lamentably misinterpreted or written off as barbaric superstition. The central point of it, as can be now seen, is the divine initiative in healing and in casting down the estranging barriers—barriers between God and man, and therefore also between man and fellow-man. Greek and Hellenistic philosophy were fully aware that there is a barrier, a separating distance, between God and man. But this was conceived in metaphysical terms—the distinction between Being and Becoming, or between Immortality and Mortality. Hebrew and Christian thought, on the other hand, have been given the insight to realise that it is still more, and more deeply, a *moral* barrier—the Holiness of God on the one side, and the sinfulness of man on the other.[1] The sacrificial rituals of the Bible were the Hebrew attempt to overcome it. The New Testament declares that the sacrifices, for all the costly devotion they commanded, were bound to be futile and inefficacious. Not only because " it is not possible for the blood of bulls and goats to take away sin " (Hebrews x. 4), but also because no human effort, however ' spiritual,' can surmount the barrier.

So far as man is concerned it is impenetrable, and nothing that we can do can take it away. It is from God's side that the rescue comes. The miracle of the Gospel of Forgiveness, as it was first preached in the ancient world, to a culture haunted by a sense of sin and of alienation from God, was that the road was now cleared and open by the condescension of God's love for man. In Christ the barriers are down ; and men are offered access to the Father, ' adopted ' into the status of sonship and enfranchised in the redeemed community. Men, being reconciled to God, could become reconciled to one another, so that the most obdurate antagonisms and group-animosities could be and were transcended. The result of accepting the message of Forgiveness was liberation into community life. The whole New Testament vibrates with this note of emancipation and release from the burden of guilt, frustration and estrangement. The Church—the Community of the Holy Spirit—in which the meaning of human life is realised in a God-centred fellowship of persons, is the direct creation of the Gospel.

It is but a few years ago that any mention of such a word as sin would have been regarded as hopelessly reactionary. ' Progress ' had left all those ideas behind ; only sour-faced, kill-joy ecclesiastics could take this depressing view of human nature. It was commonly said to be ' uncharitable ' and

---

[1] The two streams of thought begin to come together, *e.g.* in *Wisdom* II, 23–24.

often even (save the mark !) ' un-Christian ' to remind people of such unpleasant facts. This hopelessly sentimental interpretation of Christianity is not yet extinct ; and even to-day, despite all the facts, the popular mind nurtures the illusion that what the average sensual man desires or thinks is, for that reason, good or true. What frequently makes ' Leftist ' propaganda almost impossible to read is not so much the political opinions which it (quite legitimately) seeks to advocate, as its quite appalling self-righteousness. But experience is teaching us all to-day, what the high religions have always known and taught, that there is something profoundly wrong, not in circumstances alone, but in ourselves.

The old liberal faith in social progress through the dissemination of knowledge and the steady advance of ideals and enlightment was far too terribly at ease in Zion. In more than one sense it may be true that original sin destroyed the liberal party ! And indeed Europe is now finding out that without some recognition of our sinfulness the democratic experiment is unworkable. " The first universal democracy in the world was a democracy of sinners, united by their common confession of sins in expectation of the Last Judgement." [1] Where there is that recognition, there is not only equality before God, there is also a place for tolerance and pity and the give and take which is vital to democracy. If we are all sinners and fallible, " it is possible we may be mistaken." This humility is the key to freedom even in its political connotation. Where there is no awareness or acknowledgement that man stands under the judgement of God, the party will be regarded as infallible ; it will thus become intolerant and merciless and minority opinions will be liquidated.

But Democracy as we have received it, and particularly that social democracy which we are attempting to realise in this country, is impracticable unless it can take for granted

---

[1] Rosenstock–Huessy, on the political significance of All Souls' Day, quoted by A. D. Lindsay, *The Modern Democratic State.* Vol. I., p. 257.

that there is a means by which men can be delivered from their selfishness and their moral disabilities, raised to heights above their ' natural ' level and enabled to share in a common moral enterprise.   The totalitarian philosophies rest on contempt for the ordinary man.   Freedom must be able to believe in him.   Freedom in any real sense is meaningless if man is condemned to remain the slave of sin.   The presupposition of a ' free society ' is the grace of God in redemption and renewal.   This is yet one more illustration of the fact that everything in the Western legacy now presupposes the Christian religion and cannot continue to survive apart from it.

Everywhere in the world men and women are reaching after a ' social salvation,' hoping to find release from their frustration by grace of political or economic saviours.   The traditional preaching of the Gospel therefore seems to many irrelevant or meaningless.   Preachers complain of the loss of the sense of sin and try, by all the resources of their art, to deflate our pride and self-sufficiency.   Now, of course, it is true that we need to have brought home to us the depth and the misery of our predicament, and be helped to understand what it is.   Only through this radical diagnosis can we find the true ' saving faith,' and the joyful emancipation of the Gospel.   On the other hand, conviction of sin is a fairly advanced *religious* experience ;   it presupposes a vivid awareness of God and of our responsibility before him. Thus much of our preaching starts at the wrong end. The sense of sin is part of our growth in Grace, and can be left to take care of itself.   What we should lament is that people who need salvation do not know where to look for it, that in their spiritual destitution they cannot find the fountain of living waters.   The Gospel is the Gospel of God, not of man's psychological condition.

But people *are* ' worrying about their sins,' though they do not describe their predicament by that name.   The real danger is not that our contemporaries should think too little

about their moral bankruptcy but that they should become
so obsessed by it as to fall into desperation and defeatism.
The constant demand of preachers for ' penitence '—when
addressed to people who are Christians only, if at all, in the
vaguest way and do not really know what the word implies
—may easily serve to weaken morale still further.  For man
stands bewildered and ashamed amid the debris and rubble
of a world devastated by his own act.  His need and his
hunger for community have sought false and deadly satisfactions in mutually antagonistic groups—of nationalism,
class or ideology—which have turned civilisation into a desert
in which men are lonelier than before.  Hopes and ideals
seem to turn to ashes, and men are crushed with a feeling
of helplessness which breeds irresponsibility and cynicism.

As Robert Birley said in a recent lecture " the most
obvious symptom of the spiritual disease of our civilisation
is the widespread feeling among men that they have lost
all control of their own destinies " [1]  It is not only their
buildings and their prosperity but the minds and hearts of
men which have been devastated.  The world to-day is
inhabited by sick souls, conscious of inward conflict and
disharmony and of being, in some way which they cannot
fathom, out of right relation to ' life ' and the governing
forces of the universe.  This deep sense of frustration and
resentment was incarnated in Hitler and his satellites ; and
without a more radical and effective cure, based on a more
profound diagnosis, it will seek again an equivalent com-
pensation in some final revolution of destruction.  But there
are signs already that thinking people are attempting to
solve it at a deeper level.  From time to time, in the more
reflective writing, we find the use of the word ' alienation.'
There is an increasing awareness of that barrier between
mankind and the purpose at the heart of things.  Men are
being seized by the misgiving that man, who has learnt that
he cannot save himself, is left alone in his failure and defeat,

[1] *The German Problems and the Responsibility of Britain*, Burge Memorial
Lecture (S.C.M.), p. 9.

that he has been disowned by the Universe and that there is no way of reconciliation between himself and the moral law. That is, in the end, but another way of saying a fear that God has left man alone and abandoned the world to its evil and its perdition.

That is not the language used in the New Testament, but the need which it describes is identical. The need for Forgiveness—reconciliation with the Purpose of Goodness at the heart of life—is indeed precisely that need of which men are once again becoming conscious. The discipline of experience in our time may be a new preparation for the Gospel. For the Gospel declares how God has taken action to reconcile the world with his own will and to bridge that gulf which man cannot cross. If Christ died for us ' while we were yet sinners,' that means that God does not sit and wait till sinful man becomes worthy of forgiveness, but that he has taken the initiative to overcome the moral contradiction between temporal history and the eternal goodness. God has entered history to save it, to claim sinful men for his service, to set them free from bondage and despair by the manifestation of his love towards them, to give them power to overcome evil, and to raise them up into newness of life.

All genuine Christian faith in God and all hope of recovery for man are rooted and grounded in this proclamation. It is not a theory nor a speculation ; it is the telling forth of what God has done in the actual course of history in this world, through Christ's life and death and resurrection, which changes the whole human situation. ' It is not of ourselves, it is the gift of God '—a gift undeserved and unexpected, which enables men to ' trust life ' again, which lifts them out of frustration and despair and readmits them to creative service in reconciliation with his will. What the Gospel offers is not escape from the tensions and hindrances of our probation, but reconciliation in the world with the purpose of God for man and for the world.

It is, in a sense deeper than they yet know, the ' social '

salvation for which men are seeking. Christian faith and experience affirm that the liberation and renewal brought to us by Christ's life and death and resurrection are verified and operative in man through the Spirit in the redeemed community. We may say, indeed, that for the New Testament communion with God through Jesus Christ and sharing in the community of the Spirit are two aspects of the same reality. The Church is the forgiving society, in which the Forgiveness of God is accepted through a transformed relationship to man. (" If ye forgive not men their trespasses neither will your heavenly Father forgive you.") Thus the salvation promised by the Gospel is something never to be claimed by man through any purely ' devotional ' apprehension of it, and we ought never to have supposed it could be. It is not only in ' religious experience ' that the Gift of God is received ; it is verified in the Christian community ; but its influence must thence move out into secular, cultural relationships ; and only as so revealed in Christian action will men to-day believe in it or desire it.

The Church exists for the service of God's will ; and as the community of forgiven people it is the company of men and women brought into new relationship with him that they may serve his creative purpose in sanctification of spirit and belief in the truth. If the Christian religion is true, that purpose is the perfecting of persons in communion with God and one another. Therefore, the concerns of the Church on earth are as wide and as deep as God's concern for man—the overcoming of barriers and estrangements whether cultural, social or religious, the uprooting of abuses and corruptions and the setting forward of everything that is good, in the cleansing power of the life-giving Spirit and in consecration to the will of God.

For the good news is that we are not alone. The Creator of the world is its Redeemer—the God and Father of our Lord Jesus Christ, who has declared his goodwill towards us, who gives us encouragement and benediction, and in our shame does not cast us out. The permanent meaning of the

Christian doctrines which undergird and elucidate the Gospel, is that God cares for men and women ; that in their most need he stands by their side ; that the Universe is committed to Jesus, and that God has taken the cause of man for his own.

If God be for us who can be against us ? (Rom. viii. 31).

## CHAPTER V

## PRIMACY OF THE PERSONAL

THE point of breakdown in the world to-day, alike in its thinking, its ethics and its politics, is the elimination of the personal. External conditions count for more and more, personality counts for less and less. Things and processes seem to have control, and personal life is constantly invaded and occupied by depersonalising forces. It is not surprising if in this atmosphere the taste for liberty should be dying out and there should be a fatal attraction in a social and political collectivism, which lifts from the shoulders of the individual the unbearable burdens of responsibility. All this is familiar ground enough. If these tendencies are to be reversed, if men are again to become something more than statistical units in a mass-collectivism, the principle to which all our endeavours must now be geared is the ' Primacy of the Personal.' [1]

I take that phrase from Mr. Lewis Mumford, from more than one of whose fascinating books I have quoted already, with appreciation. But Mr. Mumford writes as a Humanist. Like the others he sees the point very clearly, but nothing in his mental equipment gives him the resources for getting there. So he never succeeds in becoming airborne. For this is essentially a Christian programme, and Christians alone can fully understand it. Humanists of all kinds can share in it. But the programme could never have been suggested were it not for the heritage of Christianity. It was through the faith and experience of the Church that the very concept of personality came into the Western world at all, as it is

[1] Mumford : *op. cit.*, p. 393.

within Christianity that the full significance of personal life is most clearly and deeply understood. Ours is the religion of personality in a sense that no other religion can claim to be, and this follows directly from its theology. Men to-day need to be reminded that part of what is meant by belief in God is the guarantee of personal values and the championship of the rights of persons against all that cheapens or degrades them. To that the Church is irrevocably committed by its worship of a ' personal ' God, the Father of our Lord Jesus Christ.

There is no element in the Christian teaching which is more grotesquely misinterpreted or more glibly and contemptuously dismissed. Intellectuals trembling on the brink of Theism must first dissociate themselves emphatically from this ' anthropomorphic ' superstition. (" When I say God, of course, I do not mean anything so childish as that.") The man in the street, if he reflects at all, appears to assume that ' personal ' means capricious, either in the sense of having favourites or in that of not being bound by the laws of nature —and ' science has proved ' that there can be no such Being. In other words he is making God in his own image—a finite, limited and imperfect ' person ' just like himself and the next-door neighbour. But no recognised Christian theologian has ever asserted that God is ' a person.' [1] Such a statement is utterly heretical as well as, incidentally, very silly. What theologians have asserted, and what the Trinitarian doctrine stands for, is that there is personality in God, and that in the depths of the divine reality there is that with which men and women can enter into reciprocal relationship, which can least inadequately be thus described.

The contemporary intellectual habit assumes that the disavowal of this idea is the sign of a superior mentality, while its acceptance or its affirmation belongs to lower forms of intelligence—that of the bishops and clergy for example. Yet the makers of Christian theology have not been nit-wits and ignoramuses as is now commonly assumed ; they have

[1] Cf. Clement Webb : *Problems in the Relation of God and Man.*

been trained minds, conversant with the problems and keenly alive to the difficulties involved. And this has been their considered deduction from the facts of the Christian religion. The ' terms congenial to the modern mind,' in which we are asked to re-state the creeds, are in fact at this crucial point just incompatible with the Christian world-view. The ruling dogmas of our own time, whether in philosophy or in politics, are immanentist, abstract and impersonal ; and many sincerely religious minds believe that an impersonal idea of God is more worthy of his majesty and honour than the crude and naïve language of Christians. (They frequently say that the Sermon on the Mount is Christianity enough for them, without any dogmatic overlay. One wonders at times whether they have ever read it—for it is theological through and through, and presupposes a God who is called ' Father.')

But this is a most reactionary movement. Not only does it abandon at one stroke the whole legacy of Christian thought and the ethical values which it has sustained. If it really believes that what is impersonal is more to be reverenced than what is personal, that means that It is a finer word than He. But not only is this inconsistent both with the facts of Christian experience and with the Christian philosophy of life, it is also a condemnation in advance of any stand for the dignity of persons or any attempt to recover the rights of man. What does not seem to be realised is this—that if the Church accepted this suggestion it would in that act abandon the ' Christian ethic ' and repudiate its whole social mission.

The use of the word personal in this connection is, indeed, comparatively modern. It does not occur in the language of the Bible. The Biblical phrase is, the Living God. And it can never be without misgiving that a term is adopted by theology which has no authority in scripture. (On these grounds some of the Bishops at Nicaea hesitated about the *Homo-Ousion*.) But personal is now current coinage, and though the actual word is not used, what it connotes may be said to be implied in almost every chapter of the Bible, in the creeds and in the Christian liturgies. It is in truth the fundamental axiom of the whole faith and experience of Christendom. So far from being primitive mythology, it reflects the highest level of revelation in the self-disclosure of God to man. So far from being unphilosophical, it is the most important contribution of Christianity to metaphysics. But it was not reached by speculation, it was (we may say) forced upon the Church dead against the intellectual currents prevalent in the Hellenistic age, by the facts of Christianity itself.

If in Christ God had come to men, what does this imply, both about God and man ? At least it implies that the being of God is such as to be self-revealed to man in man, and that man is such that God can be revealed in him. The whole Bible is testimony to that. Uniquely among the world's sacred books its concern is not with man's quest for God, but with God's coming into the life of man. It is not concerned with a First Cause or Absolute, but with a God who is alive and ' does things,' through which he is ever declaring himself to men. Through all the manifold drama of human life depicted in the books of the Old Testament there is always the sound of a living voice that speaks, the decision of a sovereign will that acts. There is a God of personal being, ever pressing in on man's experience, self-communicating to his people. The presupposition of the prophetic movement is personal self-disclosure through persons.

In the coming of Christ all this was verified. The whole life and teaching of our Lord reveals both the character of God and the intimacy of his dealings with us in terms that are wholly and completely personal. His use of the word ' Father ' echoes on in his own Aramaic vernacular through the Greek of St. Mark and St. Paul (Mark xiv. 33 ; Gal. iv. 6) as the characteristic note of what he had stood for. The great affirmation that God *is* love says everything that Christians have tried to say by the word ' personal '—and a great deal more. And it was, and is, through Christian experience of what Christ means in the lives of men and women, that all these new insights become possible. This defies the categories of logic and can only be expressed through ' suggestions,' in language, art, liturgy and devotion. " What eye hath not seen nor ear heard nor has entered into the heart of man— what God hath prepared for those that love him." (I. Cor. ii. 9).[1]

Moreover it is contained in this experience that this intimacy of filial relationship between finite man and infinite God, which is mediated to us through Christ Jesus, moves in the dimension of eternity. Through it new horizons are opened up. Life that consists in communion with the Living God, who speaks ' as a man speaks to his friend,' cannot be at the mercy of death. Thus there are revealed to the self new ranges of spiritual destiny beyond this spatio-temporal existence in which personal life may be fulfilled. Man's understanding of himself is thus enriched, deepened and revolutionised. It was through the inspiration of the Gospel that men began to explore for the first time the heights and the depths of human character. It gave a new inwardness to thought and life. The *Confessions* of St. Augustine are a portent of a whole new European literature. Wherever Christianity has gone it has liberated new personal energies and stood for the worth and sacredness of persons. Whatever enhances and sustains personality is the Church's friend, whatever thwarts or impedes it is its enemy. It belongs to the genius of Christianity that it operates always on the personal level. It reveals what personality really means, when the Living God through Jesus Christ is in possession of it, and how through communion with God we become in truth members of one another. It is the religion of personality actualised by the love of God through the grace of our Lord Jesus Christ in the community of the Holy Spirit.

Because of all this there has become available new knowledge alike about God and man which supplied new *data*

---

[1] Jesu  spes paenitentibus
Quam dulcis es petentibus
Quam pius te quaerentibus
Sed quid invenientibus ?

for philosophy. Christian thought has done what it was right to do, and taken the highest fact that it knows as the key by which to interpret the Universe. This was bound, when followed out consistently, to break up a philosophical tradition in which there was no room for such facts as these. This was not recognised all in a moment. When the Church first began to theologise it was obliged almost inevitably to work through the prevailing philosophies and categories of the Hellenistic world. It had to attempt to interpret its experience through the medium of an alien philosophy which, if it were the final truth about things, would have meant that this experience was impossible. For it was the limitation of Greek philosophy that it had no true place for personality nor any adequate understanding of it. All this involved the patristic theology in a certain unavoidable confusion of which the results still linger on.

The Church did not in so many words repudiate the traditional philosophy. But it transformed it from within. By its pastoral and evangelistic enterprise, by its exploration of spiritual experience within the fellowship of the new community, and by its fidelity to its own commission, it prepared the way for a new kind of thinking. It spoke the authentic language of the Gospel—that is to say, Fatherhood and Sonship. And that was not the language of abstraction, nor was it merely that of pious metaphor such as may be found in the sacred books of the East or in texts of ethnic religions. It described the essential experience of Christians. When Christ was born there occurred a unique event which can only be interpreted in its own terms.

In the end, therefore, there would be required a new and distinctively Christian metaphysic. The Christian facts cannot be fitted into any impersonal theory of the Universe. They are indeed what makes that untenable evidence which refutes that hypothesis. If God is indeed known to us in Christ, he is not an undifferentiated Absolute. It is not a ' higher ' conception of God which dismisses the Bible as

' naïve anthropomorphism.'[1] Nor is it a tenable proposition that the higher the level of abstraction and the farther the remove from the personal, the greater the intellectual achievement and the closer our approach to Reality. Some of the axioms of ' modern thought ' are contradicted by Christian experience. And indeed the very existence of the Church constitutes in effect a standing criticism of any philosophy of immanent process, operative in a self-contained system from which a transcendent reality is ruled out. For where the Church is, the Living God is ' doing things.' It is time that Christians ceased to be intimidated by a dictatorial intellectualism.

The Bishop of Birmingham, in his recent book, has made a courageous and sincere attempt to meet the ' difficulties of the modern mind ' by exhibiting the nature of Christianity within the frame of nineteenth-century Naturalism. The exhibit is so much distorted by the show-case as to become something quite different. For it is of the very essence of Christian experience that it is transcendent, ' given from above,' coming into this order from ' outside ' it. By no possibility can it be interpreted in terms of a spatio-temporal totality in which God is comprised within the cosmic process. It demands a new metaphysical category—the dynamic category of the personal. The Living God is the subject of theology, never merely an object of thought. ' No man hath seen God at any time '; no human philosophy can define him. A God defined is a God finished—he is known only through his self-disclosure. The self-revelation of God to man through Christ, in his life and death and resurrection, is an event unique and incommensurable. Either it did not

---

[1] " Christian theism acknowledges God as revealed in Jesus Christ ; and this is not the same thing as belief in absolute Being, or eternal Reason, or the Unfathomable Depth, or any other of the abstractions which in various Gnostic systems stood for God, even though such an abstraction might be called by the name of ' the first Father ' or the like, and might be held to be mediated to the world by an ' emanation ' or ' aeon ' described as His ' Son ' or even as ' Christ.' If Jesus is not the Christ, the content of the Christian revelation of God is disintegrated."—C. H. Dodd, *The Johannine Epistles*, p. 56.

occur at all, or if it did, then *ex hypothesi*, there is nothing
else with which it can be equated, no law under which it can
be subsumed.  Thus Christianity cannot be inserted into a
ready-made scheme of thought.  It must revolutionise all
schemes of thought.  And it therefore implies its own distinctive world-view, to which its own experience is the key.
Needless to say that I am not asserting that we now possess a
*summa theologiae* in which the whole field of knowledge is
embraced and interpreted by the Christian events.  It may
be that no such synthesis is possible ;  certainly in this transi-
tional age it is wholly premature to attempt it.  But we can
at least keep alive the protest.  We can at least point to the
direction in which the solution awaits our discovery.

Christian thought is through and through personalist.  It
offers, as no rival system offers, a reasoned vindication of
personality.  It is not a mythological intrusion into a
' scientific ' *weltanschauung*.  It is a world-view in its own
right.  It rests on facts.  It has been proved and tested in
the richest spiritual experience of the human race for the last
two thousand years.  The time has come when it must make
its claim.  It demands at least to be taken seriously, as a
serious contribution to thought and the understanding of the
nature of man—not to be merely dismissed by highbrows
because it throws doubt on their unexamined axioms.

This digression has not been irrelevant.  For we cannot
establish the ' primacy of the personal ' in our politics and
social planning so long as the primacy of the impersonal is
enthroned as the ruling principle in our world-view.  The
point is that Christian theology constitutes a critical criterion
which provides at once a test and corrective of some of the
prevalent intellectual fashions.  If it is true, no world-view
is tenable which regards the abstract or impersonal as in a
higher category of being or as more truly knowable than the
personal.  Why should it be regarded as more intelligent to
profess belief in a ' life-force,' for example, than to say that
we believe in God ?  Nobody has ever met a life-force, any

more than he has met ' personnel ' or ' units of school population.' What we have all met are living creatures and men at
work and boys on bicycles and schoolgirls with hockey sticks,
and so on. These are real, the others are mental constructs.
It is presumably by deliberate choice, not merely because
they cannot write English, that officials now refer to their
fellow-countrymen as though they were but entries on a
card index. It is part of the whole depersonalising tendency
against which we must now take our stand  And behind it
lies a false way of thinking which we have inherited from the
nineteenth century.

Yet all the time what we really know best, most immediately and directly, are not abstract theories but living
persons. After all, a man knows his wife far more truly
than he knows anything else—better than generalisations
about marriage. And indeed we may and must go farther
than this. Our knowledge of God is far more truly knowledge, as it is more direct and more coercive, than any other
knowledge open to man. It is not reached inferentially from
other *data*—however much subsequent reflection may ration-
alise or clarify its content. It is knowledge at first hand of
the Real because in it God is self-revealed within us ; and
in that knowledge we first know ourselves.

There are already, in the universities and at the top
intellectual levels, signs of a movement back from those
axioms which have dominated the previous generation. Far
out at sea the tide is beginning to turn. Once more the
intellectual initiative is passing back to the Church, if it will
take it. We must grasp it and not allow it to be lost again.
We must break away from the outworn dogmas of a
rationalist and mechanistic tradition, and advance towards a
' personalist ' world-view, which can by right claim primacy
for persons because a ' personal ' God is the centre of it.

If it provides a constructive critique of contemporary
trends in thought, Christianity also offers a criterion for
current political and social programmes. They can be sub-

mitted to one central test, whether they intend, and are in practice calculated, to enhance or to impoverish personal life. The test must be applied from the standpoint of the full Christian understanding of what constitutes personality— man's need for a personal community, his responsibility before God, his moral and spiritual potentialities (with the sacrifice and discipline entailed in them) and his vocation to an eternal destiny.

If we desire a community of persons, not a mass of collectivised individuals, we must be always vigilant to resist that quantitative, statistical approach which is so congenial to social planners and the bureaucracies which they create, but forgets the reality of men and women. Now the State, as centralised administration, cannot easily act by any other methods ; this is what is involved in state-action. It has its legitimate and rightful place. But when it is universally applied, as the prevalent social dogmas tend to urge, it becomes a menace to the life of persons and reduces men to the status of identity cards. (As Horace remarked, *Nos numeri sumus*). Accordingly Christian thought will be always critical of the fast-moving drift towards *Etatisme*, and perhaps there is nothing else that can resist it. By contrast, it will be jealous to insist on the rights and precious possibilities not only of voluntary social services which can still deal with people as people, but also of all the manifold varieties of non-political forms of association, whether cultural, occupational or regional, of which the State is the central organ and for which it is primarily the source of law. And among these, above all, the Family which is, both by nature and grace, the sacred citadel of personal life. There are very dangerous trends at the present moment which, by the transference of responsibility from the home to public authority, make for the undermining of the citadel. If that is surrendered everything is lost. Yet it should be obvious that the ' Christian home ' as the English people in the past have known it, presupposes the Christian religion and is meaningless without participation in the faith and worship of the Church. Here is the Church's primary contribution to the re-personalising of our society ; and without that distinctive contribution legislative action remains helpless and may even succeed in doing positive harm.

But the Church cannot live in the gaps left in the network of public social services, which will every day become narrower and fewer. It must face the entirely new situation created by the arrival of the Welfare State. Whether anyone likes it or dislikes it, the Welfare State has certainly come to stay, and in no predictable future will any going back on that be tolerated. The choice is now between a Welfare State which retains the traditions of social democracy with some degree of respect for the rights of persons, and the sole alternative which is Marxian Communism. Christians in England must make up their minds on that. They must also recognise that the possibility of retaining the first alternative in this country depends on full Christian collaboration. For us that is easier than for the Continentals. Progressive social movements in this country have been in the past inspired by the Churches, they still retain many Christian values and enjoy the support of many professing Christians. Our problem is to retain their allegiance and save them from the corrosions of secularism. In Europe, Leftist thought, broadly speaking, has been anti-clerical and anti-Christian, while the Christian front tends towards reactionism. Continental Christians have far harder choices and fearfully painful conflicts of loyalty.

To millions of men and women in this country the Welfare State seems to offer a new religion. Now at last and for the first time the whole power and authority of the State is organised for the securing of their interests. (Whether or not this will be so in fact, is one of the still unanswered questions. There are, however, ominous signs already that it may in practice result in that kind of managerial revolution which creates a new kind of privileged caste and new, and less vulnerable, vested interests.) Christians are bound, in principle, to welcome it. But they are also bound to be realists. And accordingly they must be open-eyed to the many dangers and weaknesses to which this vast experiment is exposed. Some of these are political and social ; others are moral, and they are far-reaching, threatening man's spiritual welfare.

It is, of course, being popularly said that now, since the State has taken over so much that the Church used to do in the way of social and educational work and can do these things so much more ' efficiently ' (with the public purse at its command and highly paid officials at its disposal) the Church is obsolete and no longer needed. This at once reveals a radical misconception not only of the Church's task and mission, but also of the whole meaning of the Welfare State and its moral and spiritual implications. The real fact is that the Church is needed far more, to save the new experiment from disaster. It is a truism but it is true to say that Democracy requires from its citizens a far higher standard of moral quality, more unselfishness and public spirit, more self-discipline and reliability, than any other system of government. *A fortiori* the Welfare State, which is an attempt to fashion a society of free mutual responsibility where each cares for all and all for each, must be able to take for granted in its citizens a level of character and dedication which is far beyond the reach of the natural man. If it cannot do this it must fail. The greatest need of socialised democracy is a vigorous and outward-moving Church. If this is lacking, or if it is repudiated and the attempt is made to create it in the strength of a purely secular inspiration, the whole ambitious scheme must end in failure and the Welfare State, by an ironic paradox, will degenerate into the police-state. To say this is not ' Tory propaganda ' ; it is inherent in the situation, and the Church must tell the people the truth, at whatever cost of being abused for doing so.

" The State of the future," wrote Dr. Christopher Dawson, " will not be a policeman but a nurse and schoolmaster and an officer—in short, an earthly providence, an all-powerful, omnipotent human god—and a very jealous god at that. We see one form of this ideal in Russia and another in

Germany. It may be that we shall see a third in England and America . . . we can already discern the beginnings of this paternal-democratic regime in England, and can see how all the apparatus of the social services . . . may become instruments of a collective despotism which destroys human liberty and spiritual initiative as effectively as any Communist or Nazi terrorism." [1] But this was published in 1936, and while it displays a remarkable prescience it could not, and could not be expected to, see ahead into 1948 across the convulsions of the war years. The alternatives now are not three but two ; and meanwhile, in the democratic countries, and not least menacingly in our own, the policeman-state is already above the horizon. But in essentials the prophecy is being proved true. The developments predicted by Dr. Dawson are no longer hypothetical and contingent—they are actual and they are on the doorstep.

Both for ourselves and for the whole world it is urgently necessary to avert them. For there is nothing that could do more to reinforce the prospects of recovery and restore confidence among the nations than that we in this country should provide an object-lesson in the reconstruction of social democracy and the creation of the Welfare State in faith and enterprise, freedom and magnanimity. It is not too much to say that the future of political liberty in the world depends upon it. This is the vocation which history has committed to us ; and it is a vocation which can be discharged only by a nation whose public life remains grounded in that Christian legacy from which it sprang, by which it has been moulded and by which alone its characteristic ethos can be re-created and sustained.

If, as we have argued, Christian insights into the true meaning of personality can supply a criterion for social programmes, what guidance or warning will they have to offer ? What change of direction will they indicate in the objectives of our social strategy ? We may say, perhaps, that their immediate gift will be to bring critical examination to

[1] *Religion and the Modern State*, p. 106.

bear on the true meaning of Welfare. For that in which man's welfare consists depends on the kind of being that he is.

On a purely secular theory of human nature, the content of the welfare demanded will be little more than material well-being. It will mean, in effect, the provision of ' full employment,' good wages, food, housing and social services, ample amenities and recreation. These are things which no Christian may despise. Nor can the Christian conscience rest content till this material basis of the good life has been brought within reach of all—and that not only in the ' advanced ' nations. But this alone is a slavish ideal ; a people content with such an idea of welfare may only too easily lose its soul in asking for it. For if this is all, the function of the State is just to provide the average sensual man with what he wants with a minimum of effort or corresponding service on his own part. It is terribly reminiscent of Bread and Circuses. Not only does it paralyse initiative by the expectation that ' they ' will supply everything. It opens the door to political corruption and reckless competition in vote-catching. It undermines the sense of responsibility and degenerates with fatal ease into " an ever-spreading conspiracy to get something for nothing." That was the state of affairs in the Roman Empire at the end, just before the final crash. It had so demoralised the populace that its powers of resistance, both to internal tyranny and to external enemies, had decayed. When the barbarians wanted to come, they came. It has been said that " all surrender to tyranny begins with self-corruption . . . the readiness to give up precious political rights in return for a life of undisturbed self-indulgence." [1]

But if man is in truth moral personality, this ideal is lamentably inadequate and is indeed morally disastrous. In our personal dealings with one another, in the bringing up of our children and so forth, we know very well, and act on the knowledge, that merely to give people ' what they want ' may, so far from conducing to their welfare, be the worst

[1] Mumford : *op. cit.*, p. 173.

injury that we can do them. The ' spoiling ' parent is not his child's true friend. If the State desires to breed citizens who are more than healthy and well-fed producers, who are co-operative in its tasks, who retain the hunger for freedom in their souls, it must not be a kind of universal aunt. It must so contrive that its welfare services, by protecting men against harassing insecurity and the denial of personal development by ignorance, exploitation or penury, are such as to stimulate and foster growth, and evoke the response of effort and self-discipline. Unless it is calling forth exceptional men, exceptional both in intelligence and character (not simply in knowing the tricks for ' getting away with it '), the State will be president of a human bee-hive.

Moreover the very meaning of Democracy is free co-operation in a common purpose. If the avowed purpose of society is confined to material well-being, there will be no freedom and no co-operation. A society held together by self-interest cannot be much more than a body of shareholders with a common interest in the dividend, but no other community of purpose. Unless there is conscious sharing in a purpose which transcends the interest of the individual, though in serving it he finds his own fulfilment, there will be no real principle of unity, no inward bond of spiritual cohesion. Society then will have to be held together by the ' unsanctified compulsions ' of restrictions, regulations and penalties and the apparatus of the policeman-state. The crying need of England at this moment is a cause to rally the loyalties of the people to something more than material ' incentives '—that is, in the end, a faith to live by.

If man is created in the image of God, his capacities are being undervalued, and the needs of human ' welfare ' underestimated, by the prevalent social philosophy. If it is true that the chief end for man is ' to glorify God and enjoy him for ever,' no amount of social security, no abundance of material satisfactions, can supply the requirements of his nature. All the highest reaches of personality will be left unsatisfied and unfulfilled. In any true conception of welfare there must be a central and unswerving emphasis on the realisation of the higher values and the will to promote this by the sacrifice of those that are more obvious and tangible. If people are encouraged to believe that the chief end of human aspiration is the avoidance of all pain and difficulty, all fruitful suffering or creative sacrifice, they can never rise to the stature of personality. It would of course be woolly to pretend that the mass of the people will ever be prepared for any deliberate renunciation of the lower goods for the higher ; but the example and influence of Christians must be exercised steadfastly in this direction. It may well be a special vocation for Christians to cherish an almost puritan asceticism in the laying out of their expenditure and their habits of life for the sake of higher claims. The only meaning which ' standards of life ' can have for Christians is standards of living.

The State is justified by its moral end. It exists to provide the conditions for the good life ; and there can be no good life for man, in the Christian understanding of man's nature, without conscious outreach towards God and the satisfaction of man's need for worship. It is therefore part of the duty of the State, not indeed to usurp the functions of the Church or to interfere with its spiritual autonomy, but to see to it that the Church has full scope for the un-impeded exercise of its mission. It has been said that a high review of the Church must take for granted a high view of the State.[1] That is true and it is important. But the higher the view we take of the earthly state in its responsibility before God, the more clearly we see that its God-given task, is to provide the mundane conditions for man's pilgrimage towards eternity. The State exists to safeguard religion, not religion to safeguard the State.

That this would sound absurd to the House of Commons indicates how blind we have grown to be to the hope and promise of eternal life as the meaning of the crown and the goal of personality. The contemporary Church has no task more imperative or more constructive, on all grounds, whether

---

[1] Vidler : *The Orb and the Cross*, p. 80.

cultural or religious, than its revival and re-affirmation. It would revolutionise our whole attitude to political and economic life, to education and the social services, and trans-value many of our prevailing values. In the educational field, for example, we shall see that the aim of turning out useful citizens with a ' fully developed personality ' (as the current jargon now runs) within the frame of a secular world-view is not merely inadequate, but false. For man himself is more than a citizen ; as a child of God and heir of eternal life no state may claim man entire. Personality cannot be ' fully developed ' within the confines of an earthly citizenship. Personal life can be guarded and fulfilled only when there are windows kept open from this temporal world into the eternal. " The only specifically Christian politics are the politics of the world to come, and they transform social life not by competing with secular politics on their own ground, but by altering the focus of human thought, and opening the closed house of secular culture to the free light of a larger and more real world." [1]

Here is the ultimate safeguard of liberty. If the life of men can be satisfied within the confines of an earthly citizen-ship, then there can be no effective answer to the mounting claims of the totalitarian State. If man is in truth a pilgrim of eternity, he is transcendent to the social order and answer-able at last to God alone. Why was it that under the Nazi *Gleichstaltung* scientific and cultural institutions one by one bowed the knee to tyranny, while the Churches resisted and defied it ? The survival of freedom depends, in the long run, on there being enough men and women who will say, " We must obey God rather than men."

A revived conviction of eternal life would bring back a lost grandeur to an exhausted world and fill the daily round of the common man with new zest and new responsibility. The only religion in which men to-day can find any claim or any meaning is the religion of ' social salvation.' They can hardly imagine a Church on other terms than as a means to

---

[1] Dawson : *op. cit.*, p. 123.

economic betterment, and if it cannot produce that out of a hat, or save men from the results of their own selfishness, the Church is loudly proclaimed to have been a ' failure.' They would have us identify Christianity with a secular programme of social reformation, and frankly muffle the other-worldly note in it.   But half the strength of historic Christianity derives from that which men now repudiate as irrelevant to social welfare.   The Church's power to transform this present order depends upon those other-worldly loyalties from which it draws its conviction and vitality.   It is a fact that the most dynamic influences towards political and social changes have come from the most ' other-worldly ' people.   It is a paradox of Christianity that many of those who have been most keenly aware that here on earth we are ' sojourners and pilgrims ' have been supremely the makers of history.

## CHAPTER VI

# THE REDEMPTION OF HISTORY

THE eternal Gospel is anchored in events which occurred at one point in time and space. If the Living God, as Christian faith affirms, has entered into the course of human history, then all history must be related to those facts on which the Church is founded and derive its significance from them. What Christianity claims is not only that these events are historically true, but also that they are the truth of all history, both that which is past and that which is yet to be. We are therefore committed, as I have argued elsewhere,[1] to a Christian philosophy of history. If the Christian world-view is to be commended to the minds of our bewildered generation, bruised and stunned by the impacts of history, that enterprise cannot be evaded. Yet it is extraordinarily hard to present the Christian interpretation in any way which can seem convincing to the ' climate of opinion ' in our own day. It must cut across most of its assumptions. It cannot be simply in terms of temporal process, or of what is called ' historical evolution,' since the Christian events involve, *ex hypothesi*, an invasion from a supra-temporal order. Nor can it be presented, on the other hand, in terms of philosophical idealism. For that, like Platonism (whose ghost has too long haunted our theology), cannot admit that the temporal event which is once-for-all, concrete and contingent is other than incomplete and half-real—and these are events within the time-process. He was crucified under Pontius Pilate, in Palestine, in the Principate of Tiberius.

Here indeed is the standing paradox which lies at the

[1] *Church and Leadership*, pp. 10 ff.

heart of all Christian thinking, because it lies at the heart of Christianity. It is the affirmation of our faith that these events occurring in the time-process are not drowned in the relativities of history, but are ' final,' determinative and unique. They cannot be explained in the light of other events since there are none with which they can be compared ; yet they are the explanation of all others. The Infinite is revealed in the Finite, the Eternal within the historical and temporal. This is the central conviction of the Church, and must control its understanding of history. As the Christian experience of a ' personal ' God necessitates, as was argued in the previous chapter, a new world-view worked out in its own terms, so the Christian philosophy of history will be and must be distinctively its own. There is nothing else like it in human speculation. This is its ' scandal of particularity,' and its contribution to philosophical thought. If it is ' a faith seeking a metaphysic,' it is a faith engaged in real time, and under obligation to ' take time seriously.' In the Christian incarnational world-view, metaphysics and history coalesce.

It is here alone that the answer can be found to the crux of all philosophical enquiry—how the order of super-sensual reality, the order of spirit, absolute values and *a priori* concepts of reason, can be brought into one coherent totality with the contingent world of time and change. Translated into the language of theology, that will sound less abstract and academic. For religion, the problem is to understand how God can be related to the world in such a way as not to be so transcendent that he can have no actual contact with it, nor so completely immanent within it as to be the prisoner of his own creation. Only an incarnational religion can have any effective answer to that question. " That religion (says Whitehead) will conquer which can render clear to popular understanding some eternal greatness incarnate in the passage of temporal fact." [1]

That is implicit in the Christian world-view. Yet it is inevitably paradoxical and can never be stated in purely

[1] *Adventure of Ideas*, p. 41.

rational terms. It must be presented to popular understanding in the symbols and images of religious myth. The Christian interpretation of history is suggested rather than logically stated in that mysterious and baffling element comprised within the New Testament tradition which Biblical scholars now call Eschatology—the doctrines of the End or the ' last things.'

Before the wars, this material was too much for us. It is just frankly and flatly incommensurable with views that most people then took for granted. One school of critics, led by the epic figure of Albrecht Schweitzer, found it so intoxicating that for them it came to seem alone authentic. The ' apocalyptic ' strain in the Gospel was, with whatever violence to the facts, claimed as alone genuine and true to the outlook and teaching of Christ and of the primitive Christian community. This was exaggerated and one-sided ; but it was less remote from the truth than the conclusions which most of us accepted. The majority of us went to the other extreme. We found all this so ' crude ' and ' uncongenial to the modern mind '—as indeed it is—that we wanted to cut it altogether. It was due, we insisted, to the Jewish background in the minds of the earliest believers and possibly, too, of the Master Himself. It was not much more than a *façon de parler*, something purely local and temporary, not a permanent factor in the Christian message. We wanted, therefore, to ' re-state ' all this in terms which were, admittedly, less challenging but were yet radically inconsistent with it. We used instead the language of moral gradualism— of evolution with a religious flavour. What it all permanently means, we said, is that the truth and power of Christianity will year by year grow in range and influence and the world will little by little become better till at last the Kingdom of God will be established. " Nearer and nearer draws the time, the time that shall surely be."

The strength of this ' liberal ' interpretation was that— confronted, as it seemed to be, with the choice between ' ethics or apocalyptic '—it refused, quite rightly, to abandon the ethical content of the proclamation. If that were really the choice, it chose right. But, as we can see now in the light of subsequent thought and experience, it was not. The alternatives as presented were misleading. And as exegesis this will never do. This was ' local and temporary ' with a vengeance. It is hardly too much to describe it as provincial. It was trying to fit the New Testament outlook into the frame of its own presuppositions, or, to put the same thing in another way, reading back the philosophy of the nineteenth century into the mind of the earliest Christian writers. For this was in fact the liberal creed of progress superimposed on the Biblical world-view. The course of events has meantime overwhelmed it. True, there has been a century of expansion and a marvellous advance of Christianity over vast areas of the world since men assumed, about 100 years ago, that it was already a lost cause. That is a wholly legitimate appeal, and a cordial for drooping Christian spirits. But there is another side to the picture. The expansion has not been uninterrupted. Some countries are now closed to Christianity, in others it is officially restricted, and in some former provinces of Christendom the whole power of the State is ranged against it. Nor can anyone easily maintain that there is, or has been, a steady moral progress. There has been appalling moral retrogression. Crimes and cruelties which we took for granted that civilisation had long left behind, are now so much everyday occurrences, and on so frightful a scale, that we hardly notice them. I do not see how any impartial survey could deny that during the last fifty years, in the ancient homelands of Christianity, the forces of evil have been gaining ground.

Thus preachers who still believe in Christian gradualism are finding themselves with nothing left to say beyond repeating a moral exhortation which degenerates into vague religious uplift. (" The world would be much nicer than it is ' if only ' people were nicer than they are.") But Christ did not die and rise again, the drama of our redemption was not wrought out, to support such watery sentiments as these.

7*

In this era in which we are living we can now at least understand why the Gospel has always been proclaimed not in
terms of ethical ideals, but in terms of the Cross and Resurrection. It is not the motto of an ethical society. It is a
real faith for real people in a real, and often extremely
daunting, world. What is the use of Christian ' ideals ' in
such a world as men know to-day, unless God had actually
*done* something to stamp his seal and signature on history ?
That is what the Cross and Resurrection mean. They
guarantee the victory of God's will and the reconciliation of
history through him by whom all things were made—and
that is to say, its ultimate redemption. But they give no
sanction to the creed of ' progress.'

The New Testament does not appear to look forward
through long vistas of orderly development broadening down
to prosperity and peace. Rather, it seems to expect the
exact contrary—that ' evil men will wax worse and worse,'
(II Tim. iii. 13), that there will be wars, famines, revolutions,
distress of nations with perplexity, an ever-mounting curve
of catastrophe, till the Son of Man shall be revealed. In a
sense, of course, it does not look forward at all, because its
perspectives are violently foreshortened by expectation of
Christ's imminent Coming. So far as it does begin to look
forward, it is certainly not to historical Utopias. And indeed
the whole idea of an ' evolution ' towards a perfection at
some future time, ever receding into a further distance, is
entirely alien from its thought. It understands history in
terms of crisis not in terms of gradual development. The
lines are not horizontal, but perpendicular. The crisis is
both judgement and deliverance, and every age is a ' crisis of
the world.' Here for us is the innermost truth of history—
that the world is always under God's judgement and is always
being redeemed by his power. Thus every time is a ' time
of the end.' The New Testament does, undeniably, look
forward to a climax and a consummation—as it must, if
history belongs to God and his purpose is operative in it.
But this is not within the time-process ; it is the ' con-

summation of the aeon,' as it were, the end and the winding up of time—though this can be only figurative language. Yet that ' end ' is also always present. For the kingdom of God is a present reality—not a ' far-off, divine event ' ; and the Kingdom is ever pressing in on this historical order of time and change—always here, always yet to come.

It would be hard to find anything less congruous with the modern creeds of secular Futurism than this eschatological approach to history. Whether in their liberal or their Marxian form they are ' heresies ' of Christianity, with God and life eternal cut out of it. They could only have grown up against a Christian background. The original sources of their inspiration were the biblical valuation of history as the arena of a divine purpose moving towards an end and a climax, and the Christian expectation of the Lord's coming and of an eternal hope for men and women. It is only on biblical and Christian soil that the ' golden age ' is envisaged as still ahead ; and without that bracing hope and expectation man's historical task has no incentive. But they have translated the eternal hope which nerves the faith of historic Christianity into terms of a temporal future in this world. These creeds inspired the ' century of progress ' and they are still the professed faith of millions. Dr. Julian Huxley still feels it possible, with a buoyancy that compels admiration, to canonise ' evolutionary progress ' as the ecumenical doctrine of UNESCO. It may be held with a *fides implicita* and defy the criticism of experience. But it is, at the end, at the mercy of events, and the facts now give little ground for optimism—if they do not point in the opposite direction. This secular hope, without its Christian roots, withers under the blasts of disappointment and sinks into historical determinism, or else into cynicism and despair.

In the ancient world the mystery-religions offered a privileged and private exit by which the initiated could escape from the challenge and frustrations of history, leaving the world unredeemed behind them. It would not be hard to convert men to-day to a modernised mystery-religion, Buddhist or theosophical in tendency. Dr. Huxley's brother is moving along that road and is likely to find numerous disciples. Escapist mysticism is alluring. Christians themselves have at times succumbed to it, especially when the historical situation seems to deny Christian opportunity. The more insensitive the world becomes to the recognition of religious values, the more seductive will the temptation be. But it is moral and spiritual defeatism. What we need is a faith that can overcome the world—not one to provide a religious way of dodging it. What we need is a faith which is not at the mercy of circumstances or the vicissitudes of this mortal life—a hope that is not merely wishful thinking, and a faith established in a Living God, reaching out beyond these years of time to " an inheritance which is incorruptible, undefiled and that fadeth not away " (I Peter i. 4). Such is the eternal hope of Christianity.

Yet Christianity is not ' optimistic.' The authentic Christian hope gives no encouragement to any kind of secular Utopianism. Christianity takes a tragic view of history. (Marxism is a great deal nearer to it than any form of liberal evolutionism and is for that reason a far more dangerous rival.) If, as is probable, we must now look forward to a period of radical insecurity haunted by constant danger and anxiety, and it may be even to "such tribulation as has not been since the beginning of the creation" (Mark xiii. 10)—that should be no shock to the thought or the faith of Christians. It is what they are schooled to expect—both by their reading of the Gospel narratives and by the Christian philosophy of history.

When social breakdown and collapse are threatening, then the demand for ' security ' arises as the chief and highest of all earthly goods. The safe job becomes the most desirable, and initiative is branded as anti-social. Security is what men now desire more than anything else that life can offer them. For it they will sell their freedom and independence and indeed their honour and their immortal souls. It comes to

be required of the State, as the temporal substitute for
Providence, that it should be able to guarantee security
against all the changes and chances of the world.  Men put
themselves under its protection, in return for homage and
covenanted service, as of old the little man in the countryside
put himself under the vassalage of his lord.  (It may be that
the urge towards totalitarianism is a modern development of
feudalism, in terms of an industralised society.)

They are asking for something which cannot be had and
at a price which is far too high to pay.  ' Social insurance ' is
a great ideal, which ought to be taken as far as it will go.
That the community acting through the State should do all
it can to protect its members against the arrows of outrageous
fortune—unemployment, sickness, accident, old-age—is self-
evidently right in principle as a sign and practical expression
of our mutual responsibility.  It is clearly in true line with
the Christian teaching that the strong ought to bear the
infirmities of the weak, and that we are members one of
another.  But moral and social danger begins when we blind
ourselves to its limitations.  Christians must not stand for a
confidence trick.  We deceive ourselves if we think to achieve
' security ' by any organisation in this world.  If we encourage
men in that delusion we blind their eyes to the issues of
eternity.

For this world will always be a tragic place.  Life itself
presents the demand for courage as the very foundation of all
virtue.  Safety is something that life does not offer, and
playing for safety is a slavish aim, a symptom of moral
arterio-sclerosis.  Moreover " sin reigns in the world from
Adam."  No State can give us security against sin, with the
ruin and misery it brings.  And, at the last, for every child
of man, there remains the ultimate insecurity, against which
no insurance can cover us.  We cannot be secure against
death and the final wreckage of temporal existence.  The
ultimate security is spiritual—the faith that knows that with
all its tragedy this world belongs to a true and faithful God
and that " nothing can pluck us out of the Father's hand "

(St. John x. 29). But that is something that this world
cannot give. Security in this world is a vain dream, because
it is—as Christians have always known—a world that has
been invaded by Sin and Death.

All men are sinners and all men must die. Christianity
takes these facts in bitter earnest. It can certainly never
endorse facile phrases about evil being somehow good. A
faith born in the shadow of the Cross knows too much about
it for that. What, after all, can be more appalling than the
fact that a man can destroy his own soul, and spread corruption into the souls around him, and perhaps bring ruin upon
a generation ? To call that somehow good is sheer blasphemy !
Nor is it in the least a ' Christian ' sentiment to pretend to
ourselves that death ' does not matter.' It is thought to be
' religious ' to talk like that ; but it is a false and hollow
sentimentalism and it is, to my mind, shockingly unchristian.
What can be more awful to contemplate than the prospect
of bodily dissolution ? What can seem a more complete denial
of life and love than the corpse of someone dear to us ? It is
the annihilation of everything. If anyone tells me that it
doesn't matter and that as a Christian I must not mind too
much, he simply does not know what he is talking about. I
do not believe that true Christian thinking will ever attempt
to minimise the horror of it. And in truth it is only when we
face relentlessly the unmitigated horrors of sin and death
that we can see the full glory of the Gospel or become awake
to the wonder of God's gifts—Forgiveness and Resurrection
unto life.

But when the New Testament speaks about a world under
the dominion of Sin and Death, it is thinking in wider terms
than this. It is thinking of man's historical situation, not
only of individual experience. We are in a position now to
understand what theology means by language of this kind.
It is not simply that all men and women are by the ' frailty
of their mortal nature ' prone to sin and to choose the evil.
It is rather that the social heritage is morally corrupted and

disorganised—that we are by nature children of God's wrath.[1] St. Paul's phrase the ' Mystery of iniquity ' which is, as he says, at work in the world and holds mankind under its dominion, describes something which our generation has verified. He foresaw, indeed, that evil might be personified in some one diabolic superman—the Man of Sin of *II Thessalonians*—in whom its whole power would be organised—and this, too, is something which we have seen happen.[2] But he conceives that in that satanic figure there would be signally and supremely operative all those forces of darkness and corruption, spoiling man's life and thwarting God's will for them, which are, as it were, endemic in the world. The whole world, as St. John says, ' lieth in the evil ' (I John v. 19). There is what may be called corporate sin in which we are all unwillingly partakers—though as individuals we may not be guilty—in the consequences of which we are all involved. We need no doctrine of ' total depravity ' to convince us that this is a true report of man's situation in the world to-day. We have ' been there,' we have found it out at first hand. We have known something of the moral bondage of a civilisation which has defied God. For none of us have been morally free agents. We have had to decide to do horribly evil things as the only alternative to something still worse. We have seen how what is best in natural man—patriotism, and the will to sacrifice—is corrupted and enslaved to evil ends ; and how good may be used as the instrument of evil, e.g. how the hatred of war in the democracies has served to strengthen the hands of the aggressor. We have seen one after another discovery of things which should have been for our wealth becoming fresh occasions for falling and doing foul injury to one another. The ' reign of Sin ' is no pietistic phrase, no fevered imagination of introverts ; it is the most obvious fact of man's predicament.

[1] Cf. the phrase in the Baptismal Office " all men are by nature conceived and born in sin," which is changed in the 1928 form to " prone to sin "—presumably because the older phrase is open to gross misunderstanding.

[2] Cf. the Anti-Christ of The Johannine Epistles, and C. H. Dodd's Commentary, pp. 48 ff.

And ' death reigns.' That, too, this generation knows.
" When they shall say peace and safety, then sudden destruction cometh upon them as travail upon a woman with child,
and they shall in no way escape " (I Thess. v. 3). It reads like
a sentence in the nine o'clock news. It is a fact of everyday
occurrence. This is what we have all now learnt to expect
in history infected by sin. We know that at any moment,
without warning, death and destruction may leap out upon
us from that complex of human motives, fears, antagonisms
and cross-purposes which we call the world situation, wrecking
all our hopes and good intentions, overwhelming all life and
happiness.

Of all this the Cross is the perpetual symbol. All the
failures and tragedies of history, the defeat of good intentions
and fine hopes, the destruction of what is most precious and
most god-like, are for us concentrated and embodied in the
Crucifixion of the Lord of Glory. Here is the judgement of
God on history. There is the kind of thing that history does.
This is the kind of place that the world is—for ever the place
in which Christ was crucified. Christianity has always understood this—it was born under the shadow of that Cross.
Therefore it always takes a sombre view of the prospects of
any Utopian schemes conceived by politicians or scientists to
be brought about by the agency of man. It knows too much
to believe in earthly paradises.[1] About all hopes of ' building
Jerusalem ' by those who have brought the world to its
present state it remains realistic and critical, and is fairly
open to the charge of pessimism.

But neither Caiaphas nor Pontius Pilate nor the hates and
fears and mass-hysteria which were acting through them had
the last word. " Death hath no more dominion over him."

---

[1] " Many people nowadays . . . ask us to set up a Christian society or a
Christian economic system. . . . We are indeed called on to bring about a
better society . . . to bring our institutions nearer to the mind of Christ ;
but if we think that we can produce a complete Christian model, we have
not understood Christian perfection or the meaning of the Sermon on the
Mount."—A. D. Lindsay : *Religion, Science and Society in the Modern World*,
p. 13.

This is also the world in which Christ was raised from the dead. God himself is committed to this world. God has claimed history for himself and here within it he has won the victory. Sin is defeated and death is destroyed. The Resurrection is the guarantee that history belongs to the Living God, the God and Father of our Lord Jesus Christ— not to blind fate, nor to the Devil ; therefore there is no room for despair. At the centre of history there is a ' living hope.' In its long-term view Christianity is a faith of serene and unconquerable optimism.

For it is not simply that Jesus ' survived '—escaping, as it were, from the wreckage of death. It is that God raised him from the dead. It is the vindication of God—that is, of the reality of Goodness and the invincibility of Life. The world that crucified Jesus is still God's ; he did not abandon it in its darkest hour of rebellion and disaster. The arm of the Lord is stretched forth to deliver in the triumph of the Resurrection. So it is a world that can be redeemed, and it carries upon it a grave forever empty. Life is stronger than death and good than evil.

But it is Resurrection, not survival—not a continuance or prolongation of an earthbound and finite experience, but a rising unto newness of life, eternal in quality, infinite in range, in communion with the Living God. It is the ' bringing in of a better hope.' Christian faith finds in the Resurrection evidence for the break-through into history of the ' powers of the world to come,' mastering and transforming this present world. We are not confined by the disappointing limits of our poor attainment or our past failures. Redemptive, healing and renewing forces are at work in history and in the lives of men, and there is no defeat which is inevitable. " The Lord hath smitten and he will bind us up. After two days will he revive us and the third day he will raise us up and we shall live before him " (Hosea vi. 2–3). There can be no *a priori* limits to the recuperative powers of history if the Living God is at work in it. " God gives it a body as it pleases him." The promise is not preservation or

security for that which is—the body that must be crucified—
but resurrection into newness of life.  He that sits upon the
throne says, Behold I make all things new.  And the profound
thought of the New Testament includes the redemption of
the natural order in the sweep and range of the resurrection
hope.[1]  It means ' a new heaven and a new earth.'

The Crucifixion and the Resurrection are thus always
contemporary events.  True principles and great ideals are
always being mocked, scourged and crucified ;  hopes and
dreams and moral aspirations are always being destroyed
by sin and death.  But there is never a time or a place in
which truth and love and loyalty and courage are not con-
quering lies and hate and fear, and life is not winning mastery
over death.  There is no situation which cannot be redeemed
by the mercy and the grace of God.  If the world is always
under God's judgement it can always be restored by his love.

But if history belongs to God, there mnst be a climax
and a consummation in which the tares are finally rooted out
and his sovereign purpose is regnant and complete.  It is
not to be sought in this world of time.  It is supra-historical
and supra-temporal.  It is the ' end ' ;  it is God's kingdom
come.  This transcends the limit of human thought, and can
only be conveyed to the mind through the medium of the
great Christian ' myths '—the Second Coming and the Final
Judgement.  But it is this expectation of the End which gives
to man's part in the historical drama its responsibility and its
abiding value.

History is not merely an ante-chamber, a room which
might just as well be any other room, through which we pass
on our way towards the Presence.  The historical is the
concrete actuality which is the appointed sphere of our
vocation.  History is always this history, with its given
conditions and responsibilities.  The Kingdom is ever coming
into history, but no future development of earthly history
can ever be the Kingdom of God on earth.  The value of

_____

[1] Cf. Rom. viii. 18 f.

contemporary history and its claim on our loyalty and service
rests upon our vocation to that Kingdom which is God's
reign in a restored creation.   But those who have loved and
served the Kingdom here are not scrapped in the winning of
the victory.   Their goal, their inheritance and their reward
is in the communion of the saints in light.

> Quae fessis requies, quae merces fortibus
> Cum erit omnia Deus in omnibus !

In that faith we can overcome the world, steadfast in
hope and serene in confidence, amid the instant challenge of
history " forasmuch as we know that our labour is not in
vain in the Lord."  To spread that infection of a good courage,
to resist the demoralising suggestions of apathy, cynicism
and despair, is among the most effective contributions of
Christians towards the Recovery of Man.